# Releasing the Powers
# of Junior Youth

Ruhi Institute

Books in the Series:

Below are the current titles in the series designed by the Ruhi Institute. The books are intended to be used as the main sequence of courses in a systematic effort to enhance the capacity of youth and adults to serve their communities. The Ruhi Institute is also developing a set of courses that branch out from the third book in the series for training Bahá'í children's class teachers, and this is indicated in the list as well. It should be noted that the list will undergo change as experience in the field advances, and new titles will be added as an increasing number of curricular elements under development reach the stage where they can be made widely available.

Copyright © 2006, 2014 by the Ruhi Foundation, Colombia
All rights reserved. Edition 1.1.1.PE published April 2014
Edition 1.3.1.PE January 2017
ISBN 978-958-57776-5-1


Ruhi Institute
Apartado Postal: 402032
Cali, Colombia
Tel: 57 2 828-2599
Email: instituto@ruhi.org
Website: www.ruhi.org

# Contents

## TO THE COLLABORATORS

Since its inception in the early 1970s, the Ruhi Institute has striven to serve through its educational activities young people between the ages of twelve and fifteen, often referred to as "junior youth", who represent such a special segment of society. As it witnessed the idealism and energy of so many in this age range, the Institute became convinced of the importance of providing them with the opportunity to explore a number of themes and concepts that would enable them to deal with the complexities of life, combat the forces of moral decay gaining strength everywhere, and become active agents of social change. The next several decades constituted a period of action and reflection that benefited increasingly from a worldwide experience in serving junior youth from a variety of backgrounds, including efforts in the field of development, most notably in the area of literacy. By around the year 2000, the concept of the spiritual empowerment of junior youth had emerged.

This book, the fifth in the Institute's main sequence, is intended to assist those wishing to offer the junior youth spiritual empowerment program in their villages, towns, and neighborhoods. It is the first in a series of courses, branching off from the main sequence, that will help individuals develop the capabilities required to serve this age group. While not everyone studying the book will enter this field of service, it is hoped that all will derive inspiration from the themes addressed and recognize the importance of giving due attention to the noble aspirations of junior youth—this, as an essential aspect of creating a culture that promotes attitudes towards young people so different from the ones being perpetuated in many societies today. In such an environment, then, even those not directly involved in the program will find ways of supporting its burgeoning endeavors.

Before a description is provided of the three units that make up the book, a few words should be said about the junior youth program itself. At its heart lies the concept of spiritual empowerment. Through its various facets, the program seeks to release the intellectual and spiritual powers of young adolescents and direct them towards service to humanity. The conception of power employed here differs greatly from prevalent definitions that associate it with the intention to dominate or to induce others to acquiesce to one's wishes and demands. The aim is, instead, to become channels for the flow of the powers of the human spirit: the power of unity, of love, of humble service, of pure deeds. In this connection, the program tries to engage the expanding consciousness of junior youth in an exploration of reality that helps them to recognize the constructive and destructive forces at work in society and to understand the influence these forces exert on their thoughts and actions, sharpening their spiritual perception, enhancing their ability to draw on the power of the word, and reinforcing moral structures that will serve them throughout their lives.

With this in mind, the first unit of the book, "Life's Springtime", focuses on the attributes that the Bahá'í teachings indicate are to distinguish the period of youth in general. It seeks to clarify a number of concepts related to this stage of life, particularly the interplay between service, education, and preparation for the future. From the analysis undertaken, a vision gradually emerges of the role played by each generation of youth within society, a vision that should give direction to efforts to engage junior youth in activities for their spiritual empowerment.

Among the concepts introduced in the unit is a twofold moral purpose. A dual transformation—at the level of the individual and in the structure of society—is envisaged in the writings of the Faith, and the unit suggests, in this light, that young people should be endowed with a strong sense of purpose to take charge of their own intellectual and spiritual growth and to make enduring contributions to the betterment of society. It claims, further, that these two aspects of moral purpose are complementary and fundamentally inseparable, for the standards and behavior of individuals shape their environment and are, in turn, molded by social structures and processes. Participants should pay particular attention to the sections of the unit that deal with this concept, as it is central to the discussions that follow and to the junior youth program itself.

The second unit is entitled "An Age of Promise", and it is concerned with junior youth and their immense potentialities. It seeks to consolidate in the minds of those who study it the understanding that junior youth are members of a distinct age group, one with its own particular characteristics—characteristics which leave no doubt that it would be a mistake to treat them as children. The unit also hopes to make clear that the approach adopted by the Bahá'í community towards this age group, shaped by the writings of the Faith and charged by such examples as young Rúḥu'lláh, is radically different from approaches based on prevalent assumptions and theories, so many of which propagate images of rebelliousness and crisis. To this end, the unit briefly examines the nature of early adolescence, the challenge of directing the growing awareness of young people in this age range, the effects of the environment on their lives, the concept of a "junior youth group" as an environment of mutual support, and the posture to be assumed by all those arising to serve as "animators" of such groups.

The purpose of the third unit, "Serving as an Animator", is to help participants become familiar with the various aspects of the junior youth spiritual empowerment program. Like other endeavors promoted by the Ruhi Institute, the program is offered at the grassroots of the community through a system of distance education that includes, in this case, the junior youth group, the animator, and a set of materials, which are reinforced by complementary activities. After first considering the nature of the group, the unit embarks on a discussion of the materials, the study of which represents the core of the program. Extracts are provided throughout, but two books are reviewed in their entirety—*Breezes of Confirmation* and *Spirit of Faith*—and participants will need to have copies on hand.

In this connection, it should be acknowledged that a process of moral and spiritual empowerment involves a number of interacting factors, and the greater part of the unit is given over to exploring some of these, drawing on examples from the materials, as necessary. Participants, especially those intending to enter this field of service, should recognize that there is now a considerable amount of experience in conducting the program under diverse circumstances, and what is becoming clear is the potential of the texts to empower junior youth across all cultures. The concept treated in *Breezes of Confirmation,* for instance—that if one makes an effort, one will attract divine confirmations—resonates in the hearts and minds of young people everywhere. The understanding they gain through study of the text seems to help them overcome trepidations and fears, and the lack of confidence that often accompanies such apprehension, without creating the aggressive behavior so indicative of too much emphasis on "self". In this way, the simple yet profound story that unfolds in the book, usually the first studied by junior youth, sets many on a path which protects them, at least in part, from forces of disintegration tearing at the fabric of society, forces that would rob them of their true identity as noble beings. Similarly, the clarification of concepts provided in *Spirit of Faith,* such as human evolution, to give another example, appears to assist junior youth from every culture, enabling them to reflect deeply on philosophical issues that begin to occupy their minds during this stage of life and to see the intricate connections that exist between the spiritual and the material.

Following the discussion of the materials, the unit turns to the question of complementary activities: service projects, sports, arts and crafts, and the occasional special event. As explained in the unit, much will depend on the circumstances of each group in this respect, and here the dynamic interplay between the universal and the particular is brought into sharp focus. The texts studied by junior youth address themes and concepts drawn from the writings of the Faith that, as indicated above, have demonstrated their capacity to enhance spiritual perception, develop the powers of thought and utterance, and strengthen moral structures. Yet the way in which knowledge and universal ideals find practical expression is necessarily shaped by the particular culture and the aspirations of its people. For this reason, the unit refrains from going beyond the presentation of a few principles and ideas related to complementary activities, noting that these will need to emerge in accordance with local circumstances. Nevertheless, it is hoped that service will be given emphasis in the implementation of the program, for service, it is suggested, unites the fulfillment of individual potential with the advancement of society and provides, in this way, an arena in which the twofold moral purpose mentioned earlier can manifest itself.

The unit ends by discussing several matters related to the work of the animator, sharing insights into how to go about helping a number of young people form a group, how to conduct the first few meetings, and how to converse with parents about the nature of the program and the progress of their sons and daughters. The capabilities required to serve effectively as an animator will, of course, develop over time, and those pursuing this path of service need not feel compelled, at the beginning, to offer the program in all of its dimensions. One might start by implementing the study portion only, and progressively add other elements in keeping with growing experience. It should be remembered that the materials of the Ruhi Institute are principally concerned with capacity building—a process conceived in terms of walking a path on which individuals are assisted in carrying out acts of service, gradually acquire the attributes needed to perform them, and eventually are able to accompany others in their efforts to follow a similar path.

# Life's Springtime

## Purpose

To gain an understanding of some of the characteristics
that are to distinguish youth, as a prerequisite for
engaging junior youth in a program
for their spiritual empowerment.

# SECTION 1

The period between the ages of twelve and fifteen represents a special time in the life of an individual, for it is during these years that he or she leaves childhood behind and undergoes profound change. Not yet in the fullness of youth, individuals in this age range are often referred to as "junior youth". Engaging junior youth in activities that seek to enhance their spiritual and intellectual capacities and prepare them to participate effectively in the affairs of their communities is a most significant act of service. The three units of this book focus on some of the concepts, skills, qualities, and attitudes that experience has shown are required by those wishing to implement the program for the spiritual empowerment of junior youth recommended by the Ruhi Institute.

The activities that make up the program are generally conducted in small groups at the local level. As the one animating the endeavors of such a group, you will be seen as a mentor by several youngsters who, within a relatively short span of time, will reach the age of fifteen, the threshold of maturity, when they will assume new responsibilities. In this first unit, we will reflect not so much on the attributes of junior youth but on the kind of young people that the writings of the Faith suggest they should grow up to be. What should become clear from the passages you will study is that there are a number of characteristics which are to distinguish every generation of youth and particular forces which must shape their lives. It is quite possible, of course, that you yourself are a young person in your late teens or early twenties, in which case the material presented in this unit will offer you the opportunity to examine your own goals and priorities as well.

# SECTION 2

To begin, consider the group of junior youth with whom you will soon be working. Over the next three years you will meet with them every so often as a true friend and will assist them in studying and exploring ideas together, in planning and carrying out simple service projects, and in reflecting on what they learn as a group from such experience. It would be worthwhile for you to think ahead to the end of that three-year period when they will have completed the program. The exercises below will help you to clarify for yourself the characteristics which you hope will have been reinforced in the group during that time and will have come to distinguish your young friends.

1.    Will the youth you envision be characterized by a high sense of purpose? What would they consider this purpose to be? _____

      _____

      _____


2.    On what do you hope they will focus their energies most? _____

      _____

      _____

3.    What would motivate them to work for their ideals? _____

_____

_____

_____

4.    How aware do you expect them to be of the challenges facing humanity today? Would they be convinced that they can actually contribute to making the world a better place? _____

_____

_____

_____

5.    Below are several statements that reflect attitudes towards learning. To what extent, do you hope, will your young friends have acquired the attitudes implied by each statement?

a.    They would be studious and would try to put into action what they learn.                    _____

b.    They would have the habit of reflecting on the results of their actions.                    _____

c.    They would have an open mind and would approach learning with humility.                    _____

d.    They would have an ardent desire to cultivate their capacity to serve humanity.                    _____

e.    They would yearn to achieve excellence in whatever they do.                    _____

f.    They would be passionate about the study of the sciences and the arts.                    _____

g.    They would recognize the importance of sharpening their spiritual perception.                    _____

h.    They would derive as much joy from learning to work for the progress of humanity as they would from their own intellectual and spiritual growth as individuals.                    _____

6.    Which of the following statements describe the way you hope the young people you have in mind will conduct themselves?

_____ Their standards would be more or less the same as those adopted by the generality of youth in the world.

_____ They would look in the popular media for standards to govern their lives.

_____ They would follow in the footsteps of those who strive, despite formidable challenges, to live according to high moral standards.

_____ They would be able to detect when their actions contradict their beliefs, if such contradictions arise.

_____ They would believe in such ideals as the oneness of humankind, the equality of men and women, and justice, but their actions would reflect more closely the accepted norms of a society that, while proficient in the rhetoric of such ideals, fails to uphold them in practice.

_____ They would forsake high standards in order to live comfortably in a social environment that does not uphold them.

7. Below are several questions that will help you think about the implications of a pure and chaste life. To what extent will the young people that you are imagining understand these implications?

   a. Would their conduct be frivolous? _____

   b. Would they be attached to trivial and misdirected pleasures? _____

   c. Would worldly pleasures distract them from their high purpose? _____

   d. Would they follow fashions and fads even when they are contrary to the standards of chastity? _____

   e. Would they think purity only means not having extramarital sex? _____

   f. Would they exercise moderation in the way they dress? _____

   g. Would they exercise moderation in the way they speak? _____

   h. Would they exercise moderation in the activities they pursue for entertainment? _____

   i. Would they be distinguished by their modesty and humility? _____

   j. Would they be distinguished by their freedom from jealousy and envy? _____

   k. Would they be distinguished by their purity, decency, and clean-mindedness? _____

   l. Would they be vigilant in controlling their lower passions? _____

8. Over the few years that you spend with them, how strong do you hope the willpower of your young friends will have become to accomplish each of the following?

    a. Resist temptations:               _____

    b. Overcome challenges:             _____

    c. Persevere in the face of tests and difficulties:     _____

    d. Resist pressures that require them to act contrary to high moral standards:     _____

# SECTION 3

Let us now turn to a few passages from the writings of the Faith and examine how they describe a youth. 'Abdu'l-Bahá states:

> **"O loved ones of 'Abdu'l-Bahá! Man's life has its springtime and is endowed with marvelous glory. The period of youth is characterized by strength and vigor and stands out as the choicest time in human life. Therefore you should strive day and night so that endowed with heavenly strength, inspired with brilliant motives and aided by His celestial power and heavenly grace and confirmation, you may become the ornaments of the world of humanity, and preeminent among those who are initiated into true learning and the love of God. You must be distinguished amidst men by your sanctity and detachment, loftiness of purpose, magnanimity, determination, noble-mindedness, tenacity, the elevation of your aims and your spiritual qualities; that you may become the means of exaltation and glory for the Cause of God and the dawning-places of His heavenly bestowals; that you may conduct yourselves in conformity with the counsels and exhortations of the Blessed Beauty—may my life be offered up for His loved ones—and by reflecting Bahá'í qualities and attributes, you may stand out distinguished from others. 'Abdu'l-Bahá eagerly anticipates that each one of you may become even as a fearless lion moving in the pastures of human perfection and a musk-laden breeze wafting over the meads of virtue."** [1]

1. Complete the following sentences on the basis of the above quotation:

    a. The springtime of human life is endowed with _____ .

    b. The period of youth is characterized by _____ and _____ .

    c. The period of youth stands out as the _____ in human life.

    d. During the period of youth we should strive day and night so that endowed with

        _____ , inspired with _____ and

        aided by His _____ and _____

and _____ , we may become the _____

of the world of humanity.

e. During the period of youth we should strive day and night that we may become

preeminent among those who are initiated into _____

and _____ .

f. During the period of youth we must be distinguished by our _____

and _____ .

g. During the period of youth we must be distinguished by _____

of purpose.

h. During the period of youth we must be distinguished by _____ ,

_____ , _____ mindedness, _____ ,

the elevation of our _____ and our _____ qualities.

i. During the period of youth we must become the _____ of exaltation and

glory for the _____ and the _____

of His _____ .

j. During the period of youth we must strive to conduct ourselves in _____

with the _____ and _____ of the Blessed

Beauty.

k. 'Abdu'l-Bahá eagerly anticipates that every youth may become even as a

_____ moving in the pastures of _____

and a _____ wafting over the meads of _____ .

2. You have probably heard one expression or another of the popular belief that youth should focus on having fun, for they will have to face the serious matters of life soon enough. Such a notion is clearly not in agreement with the above statement of 'Abdu'l-Bahá. What are some of the assumptions underlying this popular belief? Discuss this question with the group of friends with whom you are studying today, and write your conclusions here.

_____

_____

_____

_____

_____

_____

# SECTION 4

In the following prayer, 'Abdu'l-Bahá expresses some of the hopes He cherishes for youth:

**"O Thou kind Lord! Graciously bestow a pair of heavenly wings unto each of these fledglings and give them spiritual power that they may wing their flight through this limitless space and may soar to the heights of the Abhá Kingdom.**

**"O Lord! Strengthen these fragile seedlings that each one may become a fruitful tree, verdant and flourishing. Render these souls victorious through the potency of Thy celestial hosts, that they may be able to crush the forces of error and ignorance and to unfurl the standard of fellowship and guidance amidst the people; that they may, even as the reviving breaths of the spring, refresh and quicken the trees of human souls and like unto vernal showers make the meads of that region green and fertile.**

**"Thou art the Mighty and the Powerful, Thou art the Bestower and the All-Loving." [2]**

1.  Complete the following sentences on the basis of the above quotation:

    a.  'Abdu'l-Bahá likens those in their early youth to fledglings in need of a pair of
    _____ and asks God to give them _____
    _____ that they may _____
    through limitless space and may _____ of the
    Abhá Kingdom.

    b.  He likens those in their early youth to fragile _____
    and beseeches God to strengthen them so that each one may become a
    _____ , _____ and _____ .

    c.  He asks God to render them victorious that they may be able to crush the
    _____ of _____ and _____ and to unfurl the
    _____ of _____ and _____ .

    d.  He prays that they may, even as the reviving _____ of the _____ ,
    refresh and _____ the trees of _____
    and like unto _____ make the meads of that region
    _____ and _____ .

2.  In the prayer, 'Abdu'l-Bahá asks God to bestow spiritual powers upon youth. Which of the following do you associate with spiritual power?

| | |
|---|---|
| ____ loftiness of purpose | ____ magnanimity |
| ____ reliance on God | ____ glamour |
| ____ chastity | ____ determination to accomplish tasks |
| ____ slyness | ____ noble-mindedness |
| ____ competitiveness | ____ generosity |
| ____ solidarity | ____ desire to dominate others |
| ____ upright character | ____ firmness and resolve |
| ____ worldly ambition | ____ humility |
| ____ craving for social status | ____ pride in one's accomplishments |
| ____ love of God | ____ arrogance |
| ____ love of luxury | ____ purity of intention |

3. In the prayer, 'Abdu'l-Bahá asks God to enable youth to crush the forces of error and ignorance. Decide which of the following will assist youth in their struggle against such forces:

____ ability to discern right from wrong

____ ability to manipulate others

____ ability to express profound ideas with clarity

____ ability to recognize and overcome prejudice

____ ability to put material means to proper use

____ ability to control others in order to achieve one's personal goals

____ ability to control one's lower passions

____ ability to contribute to unity of thought

____ ability to be impartial in one's judgment

____ ability to promote justice

4. In the prayer, 'Abdu'l-Bahá asks God to enable youth to unfurl the standard of fellowship and guidance. Decide which of the following will assist youth in such efforts:

____ ability to establish bonds of friendship

____ ability to listen carefully to others

____ ability to face difficulties with calm and composure

____ ability to identify the faults and shortcomings of others

____ ability to overlook the faults and shortcomings of others

____ ability to serve society selflessly

____ ability to rejoice in the success of others

____ ability to instill hope in others

_____ ability to cooperate with others

_____ ability to promote one's own interests with little regard for the well-being of others

_____ ability to promote the well-being of the community

# SECTION 5

The quotations we studied in the last two sections give us insight into some of the characteristics that youth should possess. Clearly by the time young people reach the age of fifteen, much will be expected of them. Indeed, we know that the writings refer to the age of fifteen as the beginning of maturity. It is at this age that Bahá'í laws such as those related to prayer and fasting become binding on the individual. About the transition to maturity, 'Abdu'l-Bahá states:

> **"The suckling babe passeth through various physical stages, growing and developing at every stage, until its body reacheth the age of maturity. Having arrived at this stage it acquireth the capacity to manifest spiritual and intellectual perfections. The lights of comprehension, intelligence and knowledge become perceptible in it and the powers of its soul unfold."** [3]

1.  There are many thoughts about youth that can be examined in light of the above statement of 'Abdu'l-Bahá. Which of the following do you think apply to a fifteen-year-old person? He or she

    _____ has the spiritual capacity to reflect on the meaning of life and death.

    _____ is able to consider profound themes only if they are clothed in the garb of fun.

    _____ has the intellectual capacity to identify and analyze the forces that are influencing his or her life.

    _____ has the capacity to carry out tasks diligently.

    _____ has the spiritual capacity to overcome difficult challenges.

    _____ has the capacity to hold classes for the spiritual education of children.

    _____ has the capacity to explain the teachings and principles of the Faith with eloquence and conviction.

    _____ does not need parental support and love.

    _____ can assume responsibility for observing Bahá'í laws.

    _____ has the intellectual capacity to understand social processes.

    _____ can engage in meaningful service to society.

2.  You may wish to memorize the prayer below.

> **"O Lord! Make this youth radiant and confer Thy bounty upon this poor creature. Bestow upon him knowledge, grant him added strength at the break of every morn and guard him within the shelter of Thy protection so that he may be freed from error, may devote himself to the service of Thy Cause,**

may guide the wayward, lead the hapless, free the captives and awaken the heedless, that all may be blessed with Thy remembrance and praise. Thou art the Mighty and the Powerful." [4]

# SECTION 6

Certain physical, intellectual, and spiritual powers are brought into focus when young people cross the threshold of maturity at the age of fifteen. Required to leave the attitudes, thoughts, and habits of childhood behind, they are to cultivate new capacities. Channeling these powers into service to the Cause of God is to begin in the prime of one's youth. Bahá'u'lláh states:

> "Blessed is he who in the prime of his youth and the heyday of his life will arise to serve the Cause of the Lord of the beginning and of the end, and adorn his heart with His love. The manifestation of such a grace is greater than the creation of the heavens and of the earth. Blessed are the steadfast and well is it with those who are firm." [5]

The service rendered to the Cause by each generation of youth is indispensable to its advancement. Shoghi Effendi underscores the significance of the contribution that youth make:

> "It is on young and active Bahá'ís, like you, that the Guardian centers all his hopes for the future progress and expansion of the Cause, and it is on their shoulders that he lays all the responsibility for the upkeep of the spirit of selfless service among their fellow-believers. Without that spirit no work can be successfully achieved. With it triumph, though hardly-won, is but inevitable." [6]

As to those characteristics that make youth specially suited for the field of service, the Universal House of Justice in a message to all National Spiritual Assemblies writes:

> "The endurance of youth under arduous conditions, their vitality and vigor, and their ability to adapt themselves to local situations, to meet new challenges, and to impart their warmth and enthusiasm to those they visit, combined with the standard of conduct upheld by Bahá'í youth, make them potent instruments for the execution of the contemplated projects. Indeed, through these distinctive qualities they can become the spearhead of any enterprise and the driving force of any undertaking in which they participate, whether local or national." [7]

Complete the following sentences on the basis of the above quotations:

a.  Those who arise to serve the Cause of God in the prime of their youth and adorn their hearts with His love are _____ .

b.  The responsibility for the upkeep of the spirit of selfless service among their fellow-believers rests on the shoulders of _____
    _____ .

c. Without the spirit of selfless service, whose upkeep rests on the shoulders of young and active Bahá'ís, no work can be _____ .

d. Through the spirit of selfless service, whose upkeep rests on the shoulders of young and active Bahá'ís, the triumph of the Cause, though hardly-won, is

_____ .

e. The _____ of youth under arduous conditions and their _____ and _____ make them potent instruments for the execution of plans and projects.

f. As potent instruments for the execution of plans and projects, youth can exercise their ability to _____ themselves to local situations, to _____ new challenges, and to _____ their warmth and enthusiasm to those they visit.

g. Through their distinctive qualities youth can become the _____ of any enterprise and the _____ of any undertaking in which they participate.

# SECTION 7

A number of concepts are generally associated with the services performed by youth, among them spontaneity, excitement, and the freedom to pursue whatever possibilities capture the imagination. While there is validity in associating these concepts with service, we should exercise care not to overemphasize them. It is all too easy to fall into the habit of reducing the activities of youth to a series of exciting events and neglecting the value of understanding the nature of process and the need to learn the discipline of systematic action. Together with your friends studying this course, think of some acts of service to be undertaken by youth that contribute directly to one of the systematic processes through which the Faith advances, for example, the spiritual education of children, the consolidation of community life, and the development of human resources. Are not these activities conducive to joy? Do they not allow for the appropriate degree of spontaneity?

_____

_____

_____

_____

_____

_____

_____

_____

_____

_____

_____

_____

# SECTION 8

We often hear that the period of youth is a time of preparation. This statement is true indeed. Referring to the changes needed in the world today, the Universal House of Justice writes that "the transformation which is to occur in the functioning of society will certainly depend to a great extent on the effectiveness of the preparations the youth make for the world they will inherit." What we should ask, then, is how young people can best prepare themselves for the responsibilities they will have to shoulder.

Not infrequently, this question gives rise to others concerning the relationship between studies—whether academic, vocational, or professional—and service to the Faith. Specifically, it is sometimes not clear how much energy young people should devote to each. One extreme is to advise youth to dedicate themselves fully to their education and to wait until they have gained more life experience before becoming seriously engaged in one or more areas of service. The other extreme is to encourage them to forgo any formal education and to spend their energies, especially at this time of opportunity, entirely in the field of service. Both of these extremes, of course, should be avoided. Below are a few quotations from the writings to help you think through this set of issues.

That service should be central to the life of every youth is clear from many passages, such as the following written on behalf of the Guardian:

> **"The youth should become severed from all things of the world and, filled with the dynamic power of the Holy Spirit, arise to spread the Message and quicken the hearts."** [8]

This next passage written on behalf of Shoghi Effendi refers to the need for youth to develop their intellectual and spiritual capacities as part of their preparation for the future:

> **"His hope, as well as that of the friends, is that you should increase both in number and spirituality. The future of this Cause, which is so dear to us all, depends upon the energy and devotion of the rising generation. It is you who before long will be called to shoulder its responsibilities and undertake its spread. To do that, however, you ought to be well equipped. You ought to have your intellectual as well as spiritual side equally developed."** [9]

A letter written by the Universal House of Justice further explains:

> **"For any person, whether Bahá'í or not, his youthful years are those in which he will make many decisions which will set the course of his life. In these years he is most likely to choose his life's work, complete his education, begin to earn his own living, marry and start to raise his own family. Most important**

of all, it is during this period that the mind is most questing and that the spiritual values that will guide the person's future behavior are adopted." [10]

And another letter written on behalf of the House of Justice provides the following relevant guidance:

"Many youth have found that dedicating a period of service to the Faith, either in their own countries or abroad, is an excellent means of gaining knowledge and experience, setting the stage for a life of devotion to the Cause. However, care should be taken to ensure that, in an effort to help youth reach greater heights of service, they are not prompted to disregard the need to prepare themselves for the future. A period of full-time service to the Faith can, of course, be a valuable component of their preparation. Whether they are at a point in their studies or careers where they can undertake such a service is a matter which has to be determined on a case-by-case basis, through consultations with parents, friends and the institutions of the Faith. In all cases, obtaining an education within one's range of possibilities and acquiring a trade or profession with which to earn one's livelihood must be given due importance. Yet to define the fruitful years of youth exclusively as a stage of preparation would be to overlook the creative energies which are available to youth in such abundance. After all, so many of the early heroes of the Faith were young men and women who arose to accomplish the greatest of deeds in the path of their Beloved." [11]

Now, write a brief statement that reflects your understanding of what it means for the period of youth to be a time of preparation.

# SECTION 9

No doubt the statement you wrote in the last section stresses how important it is for youth to prepare themselves adequately for the world they will inherit by receiving an academic education or training in a vocation or profession. But you surely also noted that service to the Cause cannot be "put on hold" while one studies. Such an attitude tends to perpetuate itself into the future as one gets older, and one can end up waiting all one's life for the right conditions in order to begin to serve in earnest. This view of the relationship between studies and service can arise when education is defined in terms of book learning alone. When instead we see service as an arena in which knowledge is applied and the intellect developed, this kind of thinking is readily avoided, and service is considered not only part of, but central to, any sound process of preparation for the future. Indeed, when service to the Cause begins in the prime of one's youth, it becomes a guiding principle throughout all of life, enabling one to chart a proper course and keep one's direction clear.

This realization leads naturally to questions about the kind of preparation youth require to enhance their capacity for service. It would be easy to think that, by attending the various gatherings of the Bahá'í community, including those which satisfy their natural desire to have fun together, young people will develop their capacities and prepare themselves adequately for a life of service. Yet the writings suggest that such an informal educational process, while necessary, is not sufficient.

If we look carefully at his communications, we see that Shoghi Effendi expresses the hope that youth will become "well educated and trained" in the teachings and will acquire a "thorough" and "sound" knowledge of the Faith. In addition, he encourages them to learn through "active, wholehearted and continued participation" in the activities of their communities. In this connection, he explains that community life provides "an indispensable laboratory," where young people can "translate into living and constructive action the principles" they glean from study of the Faith. It is in "becoming a real part of that living organism", he indicates, that they can "catch the real spirit which runs throughout the Bahá'í Teachings". Thus, a formal educational process is needed to help young people equip themselves for service, one that is embedded in the reality of community life. Activity for the sake of activity, study for the sake of study, does not meet the requirement.

Many messages of the Universal House of Justice speak in similar terms. Understanding increases greatly, one message makes clear, "when study and service are joined and carried out concurrently". "There, in the field of service, knowledge is tested, questions arise out of practice, and new levels of understanding are achieved." In countries across the globe training institutes have been established for the explicit purpose of developing the human resources of the Cause through a formal course of study. Growing numbers of people everywhere are engaged in a systematic educational process to increase their capacity for service, and youth have consistently remained in the forefront of this process of preparation. Regarding the agency of the training institute, one letter written on behalf of the House of Justice explains:

> **"It strives to engage the individual in an educational process in which virtuous conduct and self-discipline are developed in the context of service, fostering a coherent and joyful pattern of life that weaves together study, worship, teaching, community building and, in general, involvement in other processes that seek to transform society. At the heart of the educational process is contact**

with the Word of God, whose power sustains every individual's attempts to purify his or her heart and to walk a path of service with 'the feet of detachment'." [12]

Another letter written on behalf of the House of Justice states:

". . . the courses of the institute are intended to set the individual on a path in which qualities and attitudes, skills and abilities, are gradually acquired through service—service intended to quell the insistent self, helping to lift the individual out of its confines and placing him or her in a dynamic process of community building." [13]

And, referring to the contingents of young people around the world, the House of Justice writes:

"Irrespective of particulars, they will, one and all, share in the desire to dedicate their time and energy, talents and abilities, to service to their communities. Many, when given the opportunity, will gladly devote a few years of their lives to the provision of spiritual education to the rising generations. In the young people of the world, then, lies a reservoir of capacity to transform society waiting to be tapped. And the release of this capacity should be regarded by every institute as a sacred charge." [14]

# SECTION 10

As we saw in the two preceding sections, we have to be mindful when considering any situation not to break it apart in such a way that we begin to compartmentalize aspects of our lives, which can lead to unnecessary contradictions. In general, the human mind has a tendency to fragment the world it encounters. Reality—physical, social, and spiritual—is too vast to be understood in its entirety. It is not unreasonable, then, to break it up in order to understand it in parts. However, when this is done without taking into account the wholeness of reality, difficulties arise. Conflicts among people of different races, colors, nationalities, and religions are examples of some of the problems that can emerge from a fragmented conception of existence—for the oneness of humanity is real, and its division along racial, ethnic, and national lines a product of the human mind and the result of historical circumstances.

If we are not careful and end up adopting such a fragmented approach to our lives, we can create all kinds of dichotomies that are largely imaginary. Work, leisure, family life, spiritual life, physical health, intellectual pursuits, individual development, collective progress, and so on become pieces that together make up our existence. When we accept such divisions as real, we feel pulled in many directions, trying to respond to what we consider to be the demands of these different facets of life. We are bewildered by apparently conflicting aims: Should I sacrifice my family life to serve the Cause? Will not serving the Faith interfere with my efforts to raise my children? These are two examples of the myriad of questions that can arise.

To resolve the dichotomies we have created, we sometimes try to divide our time equally among the various demands placed on us. On other occasions, we attempt to prioritize responsibilities and focus our energies on those we believe to be the most important at any particular moment. A careful allotment of time and energy is of course necessary. But it is only fruitful when we remain conscious of the interconnectedness of the many aspects of our lives. If we fail to see the whole, the tension created among all the parts can give rise to anxiety and even confusion.

Below are various aspects of life placed in pairs that should reinforce each other, but which are sometimes thought to be in conflict. For every sentence that follows each pair, decide whether it represents the kind of thinking that is conducive to an integrated way of life or whether it is indicative of a tendency towards fragmentation. Mark it with an "I" or "F" accordingly.

1.  Family and work

    _____ My family life will suffer if I work hard at my job.

    _____ I often discuss with my family my accomplishments at work and the challenges I face there.

    _____ Of course women can excel in their careers, but the children always pay the price.

    _____ If I want to raise my children well, I will have to forget about my profession.

    _____ I can achieve excellence in my profession and conscientiously attend to my family responsibilities.

2.  Education and service to the Cause

    _____ Academic achievement is a prerequisite for entering the field of service.

    _____ The knowledge we acquire through our studies is an asset in the field of service, and the experience we gain in the arena of service deepens our knowledge.

    _____ We have to abandon our studies if we really want to devote ourselves to the Cause.

    _____ One of our greatest aspirations is to study the teachings of the Faith and learn to apply them in endeavors that promote the betterment of the world.

    _____ The period of service that we dedicate to promoting the well-being of our communities will assist us in choosing suitable fields of study.

3.  Intellectual development and the development of spiritual qualities

    _____ The independent investigation of truth requires the cultivation of the intellect as well as the acquisition of spiritual qualities.

    _____ Intellectual development requires justice, honesty, and lack of prejudice.

_____ To develop spiritually, one has to let go of one's intellect.

_____ Our minds and hearts are not separate from each other; they represent complementary and mutually interactive aspects of one reality—our soul.

_____ Spiritual qualities are developed through conscious knowledge and the exercise of good deeds.

4.    Material life and spiritual life

_____ We must deny ourselves material pleasure in order to develop spiritually.

_____ Spiritual matters should be put aside until we are old; during our youth we should take advantage of every opportunity to advance materially.

_____ The material needs of people have to be satisfied before they are ready to pay attention to spiritual matters.

_____ The purpose of life on this material plane is to develop spiritual qualities and powers.

_____ We should enjoy all the bounties that the world has to offer but should not allow earthly desires to take hold of our hearts and prevent us from drawing nearer and nearer to God.


# SECTION 11

In this unit we are considering not so much the attributes that define junior youth but the characteristics of the young men and women that the writings suggest they should grow up to be. We began this exploration by looking at two quotations that gave us insights into some of these characteristics. We then saw that the age of fifteen marks a special point in the life of an individual, for it represents the threshold of maturity, a time when new powers and capacities are brought into focus. We know what a significant role young people can play in the life of the Cause and how important it is for their tremendous capacities to be directed towards service to humanity. We have also acknowledged the need for youth to consciously prepare themselves for their future life and have seen that service itself is essential to such preparation, as are their studies—both those needed to acquire the knowledge and skills to earn a livelihood and those that will enhance their capabilities to render service to their communities.

You may find it useful to pause here and reflect on what you have studied up to this point. Below are several statements. Read each one and decide whether it is true or false. Although the answer in some cases may be obvious, we hope that you will give the overall exercise adequate attention. It is intended to take you through a sequence of ideas which will help you to organize your thoughts about the material we have covered so far.

a.   For an individual, turning fifteen means reaching the age of maturity, but this is more of a symbolic mark and does not affect his or her life in any meaningful way.                    T ☐ F ☐

b.  Most youth are immature and cannot assume major responsibilities; they are easily distracted and cannot be relied upon.                                          T ☐  F ☐

c.  Youth are eager to assume responsibility for the work of the Faith, but because of their inexperience and immaturity, they are unable to accomplish a great deal.                    T ☐  F ☐

d.  When a young person reaches the age of maturity, he or she can take on more responsibilities in some areas of life, but not in others.                                      T ☐  F ☐

e.  Youth have the potential needed to arise and serve the Faith with constancy and selflessness.                     T ☐  F ☐

f.  Youth can show forth the willpower and dedication needed to engage in systematic action in service to the Faith.       T ☐  F ☐

g.  Those who arise to serve the Cause in the prime of their youth are greatly blessed.                              T ☐  F ☐

h.  Youth should focus most of their attention on their studies; their extra time can be devoted to service.            T ☐  F ☐

i.  Without receiving the highest levels of academic training, youth cannot serve society effectively.                 T ☐  F ☐

j.  All fields of human endeavor are open to youth; they should choose those suited to their talents and circumstances, enter them in a spirit of service, and strive for excellence.      T ☐  F ☐

k.  Youth do not have enough experience and knowledge to engage in meaningful conversation about the Faith with those they encounter; it is best they serve in other ways.          T ☐  F ☐

l.  Youth do not have the experience and knowledge needed to engage in meaningful conversation about the Faith with those they encounter and should be encouraged, instead, to simply show forth exemplary conduct.                   T ☐  F ☐

m.  Youth have great potential to understand the teachings brought by Bahá'u'lláh and to share them with their peers.   T ☐  F ☐

n.  Youth have great potential to understand the teachings brought by Bahá'u'lláh and to share them with people from all walks of life, both young and old.                      T ☐  F ☐

o.  Youth are eager to acquire the knowledge and abilities needed to share the teachings of the Faith with others.      T ☐  F ☐

p. Youth are among the greatest resources of the Cause of God and should be helped, through a proper course of study and constant encouragement, to become capable of serving their communities and humanity.    T ☐   F ☐

q. Youth require special activities that allow them to have fun; it is difficult for them to be serious over an extended period of time.    T ☐   F ☐

r. Learning to be systematic comes later in life, when spontaneity has run out.    T ☐   F ☐

s. The ability of youth to endure arduous conditions and to adapt to new situations opens to them many avenues of service.    T ☐   F ☐

t. Youth have the power to overcome difficulties by exemplifying in their lives the high moral standards set forth in the teachings.    T ☐   F ☐

u. Youth have inquisitive minds and can find answers to their questions by participating fully in the life of the community.    T ☐   F ☐

v. It is the youth who contribute decisively to the vigor and the purity of the Bahá'í community and can become its driving force.    T ☐   F ☐

w. The great potentialities latent within the Bahá'í community can unfold through the spirit of selfless service demonstrated by youth.    T ☐   F ☐

# SECTION 12

It is hoped that the exercise in the last section helped you to consolidate your thinking about the period of youth and that the image you have acquired of this stage of life is one of active service, combined with rigorous preparation for the future. Let us consider this theme further.

The interplay we have discussed between service, education, and preparation needs to unfold within a particular context. Specifically, it should contribute to two processes of transformation envisioned in the writings of the Faith: the pronounced intellectual and spiritual growth of the individual and the transformation of society. We know that "the supreme and distinguishing function" of Bahá'u'lláh's Revelation is "none other than the calling into being of a new race of men," and every Bahá'í strives daily to align his or her thoughts and actions with those of the individual we see depicted in the Sacred Text. The writings emphasize an equally profound transformation in the structure of society. "Soon will the present-day order be rolled up," Bahá'u'lláh tells us, "and a new one spread out in its stead." "All men", He declares, "have been created to carry forward an ever-advancing civilization."

This dual transformation will only occur through conscious effort, and it is essential that young people realize its implications for their lives and become endowed with a strong sense of purpose, both to take charge of their own personal growth and to contribute to the transformation of society. Such a twofold moral purpose will naturally find expression in a life of service.

The following quotations shed light on one aspect of this sense of moral purpose—related to our own intellectual and spiritual growth:

> **"The purpose of the one true God in manifesting Himself is to summon all mankind to truthfulness and sincerity, to piety and trustworthiness, to resignation and submissiveness to the Will of God, to forbearance and kindliness, to uprightness and wisdom. His object is to array every man with the mantle of a saintly character, and to adorn him with the ornament of holy and goodly deeds."** [15]

> **"The foundation-stone of a life lived in the way of God is the pursuit of moral excellence and the acquisition of a character endowed with qualities that are well-pleasing in His sight."** [16]

> **"It is given to man to obtain knowledge, to attain to great spiritual perfection, to discover hidden truths and to manifest even the attributes of God."** [17]

> **"The purpose of God in creating man hath been, and will ever be, to enable him to know his Creator and to attain His Presence."** [18]

1. Complete the following sentences on the basis of the above quotations:

   a. The purpose of the one true God in manifesting Himself is to summon all mankind to _____

   _____

   _____

   _____ .

   b. God's object is to array every man with _____

   _____ , and to adorn him with _____

   _____ .

   c. The foundation-stone of a life lived in the way of God is _____

   _____ and _____

   _____

   _____ .

d.　It is our duty to obtain _____ , to attain _____

　　　　_____ , to discover _____

　　　　and to manifest _____ .

　　e.　The purpose of God in creating us has been, and will ever be, to _____

　　　　_____ and to _____

　　　　_____ .

2.　　Having a vision of the possibilities inherent in the human soul is important to an individual's sense of purpose. In what way are the two connected? _____

　　　　_____

　　　　_____

3.　　An individual's sense of purpose is reinforced by the knowledge that this earthly life is but a small part of an eternal journey towards the presence of God. Can you explain why? _____

　　　　_____

　　　　_____

　　　　_____

　　The next set of quotations shed light on the other aspect of this sense of moral purpose, that is, to contribute to the transformation of society:

> **"This Wronged One testifieth that the purpose for which mortal men have, from utter nothingness, stepped into the realm of being, is that they may work for the betterment of the world and live together in concord and harmony."** [19]

> **"And the honor and distinction of the individual consist in this, that he among all the world's multitudes should become a source of social good. Is any larger bounty conceivable than this, that an individual, looking within himself, should find that by the confirming grace of God he has become the cause of peace and well-being, of happiness and advantage to his fellow men? No, by the one true God, there is no greater bliss, no more complete delight."** [20]

> **"How excellent, how honorable is man if he arises to fulfill his responsibilities; how wretched and contemptible, if he shuts his eyes to the welfare of society and wastes his precious life in pursuing his own selfish interests and personal advantages."** [21]

> **"Do not busy yourselves in your own concerns; let your thoughts be fixed upon that which will rehabilitate the fortunes of mankind and sanctify the hearts and souls of men."** [22]

> **"They who are the people of God have no ambition except to revive the world, to ennoble its life, and regenerate its peoples."** [23]

1.　　Complete the following sentences on the basis of the above quotations:

a. The purpose for which we have, from utter nothingness, stepped into the realm of being, is that we may _____ _____ and _____ _____ .

b. The honor and distinction of the individual consist in this, that _____ _____ _____ .

c. There is no larger bounty conceivable than that an individual, looking within himself, should find that by _____ he has become _____ _____ _____ .

d. How honorable is man if he arises to _____ ; how wretched and contemptible, if he shuts his eyes to _____ _____ and _____ _____ _____ .

e. We should not busy ourselves in _____ , but should fix our thoughts on that which will _____ _____ _____ .

f. They who are the people of God have no ambition except to _____ _____ , to _____ , and _____ _____ .

2. Having a vision of the great opportunities open to humanity at this stage of development, when its unification into one common family is a real possibility, is important to an individual's sense of purpose. In what way are the two connected? _____
_____
_____

3. An individual's sense of purpose is reinforced by the knowledge that humanity is on a long evolutionary path leading to a Divine civilization. Can you explain why? _____
_____
_____

# SECTION 13

As suggested by the exercises in the last section, an understanding of the nature of the change in the individual and in society set forth in the writings is fundamental to the sense of purpose that young people should possess. To acquire the gemlike qualities that "lie hidden within the mine of their true and inmost selves" and to contribute to the creation of a materially and spiritually prosperous world civilization, they must appreciate the magnitude of the transformation called for by Bahá'u'lláh. Of course, people everywhere speak about the need for change today. What we should realize is that the transformation destined to occur in the individual and society under the direct influence of Bahá'u'lláh's Revelation is far greater than what most people would even imagine possible.

Let us try to get a glimpse into the magnitude of the change that will occur at the level of the individual by reflecting on several quotations. Bahá'u'lláh tells us:

> "A race of men, incomparable in character, shall be raised up which, with the feet of detachment, will tread under all who are in heaven and on earth, and will cast the sleeve of holiness over all that hath been created from water and clay." [24]

And in one passage He declares:

> "Say: He is not to be numbered with the people of Bahá who followeth his mundane desires, or fixeth his heart on things of the earth. He is My true follower who, if he come to a valley of pure gold, will pass straight through it aloof as a cloud, and will neither turn back, nor pause. Such a man is, assuredly, of Me. From his garment the Concourse on high can inhale the fragrance of sanctity." [25]

In another passage He states:

> "The companions of God are, in this day, the lump that must leaven the peoples of the world. They must show forth such trustworthiness, such truthfulness and perseverance, such deeds and character that all mankind may profit by their example." [26]

And He further explains:

> "Within the very breath of such souls as are pure and sanctified far-reaching potentialities are hidden. So great are these potentialities that they exercise their influence upon all created things." [27]

'Abdu'l-Bahá tells us:

> "O ye friends of God! Make ye a mighty effort that all the peoples and kindreds of the world, even the enemies, should put their trust, confidence and hope in you. Should a soul commit a hundred thousand misdeeds, yet may he hope for forgiveness and may not become despondent or grieved. Such is the conduct and behavior of the people of Bahá. Such is the foundation of the path of loftiness. Let your conduct and manners conform to the counsels of 'Abdu'l-Bahá." [28]

The splendor of the attributes that will characterize this new human being, as described in the writings, is dazzling, and we are overwhelmed by the glimpses we get of the powers and capacities of this "new race of men". Upon reading such passages we could react in different ways. We might be inclined to think the standard set by the writings is so far beyond our reach that it is futile to try too hard to live by it and, as a result, slip into mediocrity; in such a state, we allow ourselves to be lulled into believing it is sufficient to simply avoid unseemly conduct. When one is endowed with a strong sense of purpose, however, passages like those above are a constant source of encouragement and spur one on to greater heights.

Yet we are also blessed with another source of inspiration in the person of 'Abdu'l-Bahá, the perfect Exemplar of His Father's teachings. Though conscious that 'Abdu'l-Bahá moves in a sphere of His own and that no human being can ever hope to attain His exalted station, we see in Him the embodiment of every Bahá'í ideal and strive towards the standard of conduct which He exemplified. You and your friends studying this course may find it helpful to choose phrases from the above quotations and think of episodes from 'Abdu'l-Bahá's life that reflect the qualities mentioned in each. For example, when we try to envision walking with "the feet of detachment", stories from His life come to mind that show us what it means to go through this world detached from all created things. When we think of "the fragrance of sanctity", we know that it is from His "garment" that the "Concourse on high" could inhale its sweetness, and we remember stories that illustrate His utter sanctity.


# SECTION 14

Now let us consider the profound process of transformation that must occur at the level of society. Bahá'u'lláh states:

> **"By My Self! The day is approaching when We will have rolled up the world and all that is therein, and spread out a new order in its stead."** [29]

He tells us further:

> **"The world's equilibrium hath been upset through the vibrating influence of this most great, this new World Order. Mankind's ordered life hath been revolutionized through the agency of this unique, this wondrous System—the like of which mortal eyes have never witnessed."** [30]

And 'Abdu'l-Bahá affirms:

> **"Justice and truth will encompass the world; enmity and hatred will disappear; all causes of division among peoples, races and nations will vanish; and the cause of union, harmony and concord will appear. The negligent will awake, the blind will see, the deaf will hear, the dumb will speak, the sick will be cured, the dead will arise. War will give place to peace, enmity will be conquered by love, the causes of dispute and wrangling will be entirely removed, and true felicity will be attained. The world will become the mirror of the Heavenly Kingdom; humanity will be the Throne of Divinity."** [31]

On another occasion He explains:

> **"That which was applicable to human needs during the early history of the race could neither meet nor satisfy the demands of this day and period of newness and consummation. Humanity has emerged from its former degrees of limitation and preliminary training. Man must now become imbued with new virtues and powers, new moralities, new capacities. New bounties, bestowals and perfections are awaiting and already descending upon him."** [32]

And He exhorts us:

> **". . . we must strive with heart and soul in order that this darkness of the contingent world may be dispelled, that the lights of the Kingdom shall shine upon all the horizons, the world of humanity become illumined, the image of God become apparent in human mirrors, the law of God be well established and that all regions of the world shall enjoy peace, comfort and composure beneath the equitable protection of God."** [33]

As in the case of the individual, it is difficult for us to imagine the full splendor of the civilization destined to come into being. Indeed, it would hardly be possible to describe its features. Yet we cannot be so overwhelmed by the magnitude of the transformation required that we think it will occur magically, without effort on our part. Our eyes should remain fixed on Bahá'u'lláh's World Order, and we should recognize that even the smallest act can contribute towards its construction. To reflect further on the extent of the change that will take place in society, fill in the blanks in each of the sentences below, using one of the following words or phrases:

> disappear, vanish, give place, spread out, illumined,
> established, conquered, removed, attained, dispelled,
> rolled up, encompass, appear, enjoy, become, shine

a.  The day is approaching when the world and all that is therein will be _____ _____ .

b.  The day is approaching when a new order will be _____ in place of the present one.

c.  Justice and truth will _____ the world.

d.  Enmity and hatred will _____ .

e.  All causes of division among peoples, races, and nations will _____ .

f.  The cause of union, harmony, and concord will _____ .

g.  War will _____ to peace.

h.  Enmity will be _____ by love.

i.  The causes of dispute and wrangling will be entirely _____ .

j.  True felicity will be _____ .

k.  The world will _____ the mirror of the Heavenly Kingdom.

l.  The darkness of the contingent world will be _____ .

m.  The lights of the Kingdom will _____ upon all the horizons.

n.  The world of humanity will become _____ .

o.  The law of God will be well _____ .

p.  All regions of the world will _____ peace, comfort, and composure beneath the equitable protection of God.


# SECTION 15

The passages and exercises in the last two sections have given us insight into the profound transformation that will take place in the individual and in society as a result of Bahá'u'lláh's Revelation. To consider further the magnitude of the transformation He has envisioned, read the statements below. Each one expresses some praiseworthy attribute of the individual or society such as justice, fairness, or loving-kindness. Yet the passages in the preceding sections leave little doubt that Bahá'u'lláh has called humanity to a much higher standard of individual and collective conduct. Try to rephrase each of the sentences so that it illustrates more closely the standard set by His Revelation. An example for the first statement is provided to assist you.

a.  One must control one's feelings of jealousy and not be consumed by them.

b.  We should blot out from our hearts the slightest trace of jealousy and feel sincere joy in the achievements of others.

a.  It is enough to be courteous to everyone we meet, whether friend or stranger.

b.  _____

_____


a.  We should be thankful for the material wealth God has given to us and always contribute to charities when asked.

b.  _____

_____


a.  One should strive not to enter into conflict with others.

b.  _____

_____

a.  To live a moral life implies that we should not cause harm to anyone.

b.  _____

_____

a.  To live in peace, we should learn to tolerate peoples of diverse cultures, backgrounds, and religions.

b.  _____

_____

a.  People should learn to stand up for their rights.

b.  _____

_____

a.  It is imperative for governments to dedicate the resources needed to create the best programs possible for schools that are training the minds of our future leaders.

b.  _____

_____

a.  Prisons should be modernized in order to rehabilitate criminals.

b.  _____

_____

Now reflect on the sentences you have written in light of the passages below. The first one helps us to think about how purified of earthly desires hearts must be:

**"O Son of Earth! Know, verily, the heart wherein the least remnant of envy yet lingers, shall never attain My everlasting dominion, nor inhale the sweet savors of holiness breathing from My kingdom of sanctity."** [34]

Regarding the way we should treat one another, the following quotation offers some insight:

**"So intense must be the spirit of love and loving kindness, that the stranger may find himself a friend, the enemy a true brother, no difference whatsoever existing between them."** [35]

This quotation sheds light on proper attitudes towards giving:

**"O Children of Dust! Tell the rich of the midnight sighing of the poor, lest heedlessness lead them into the path of destruction, and deprive them of the Tree of Wealth. To give and to be generous are attributes of Mine; well is it with him that adorneth himself with My virtues."** [36]

Concerning the nature of our interactions with others, we read:

"Be thou a summoner to love, and be thou kind to all the human race. Love thou the children of men and share in their sorrows. Be thou of those who foster peace. Offer thy friendship, be worthy of trust. Be thou a balm to every sore, be thou a medicine for every ill. Bind thou the souls together. Recite thou the verses of guidance. Be engaged in the worship of thy Lord, and rise up to lead the people aright. Loose thy tongue and teach, and let thy face be bright with the fire of God's love. Rest thou not for a moment, seek thou to draw no easeful breath. Thus mayest thou become a sign and symbol of God's love, and a banner of His grace." [37]

And, on the question of moral behavior, we are advised:

"The days when idle worship was deemed sufficient are ended. The time is come when naught but the purest motive, supported by deeds of stainless purity, can ascend to the throne of the Most High and be acceptable unto Him." [38]

As for the treatment of people of different backgrounds, this passage provides us with insight:

"Consort with all the peoples, kindreds and religions of the world with the utmost truthfulness, uprightness, faithfulness, kindliness, goodwill and friendliness, that all the world of being may be filled with the holy ecstasy of the grace of Bahá, that ignorance, enmity, hate and rancor may vanish from the world and the darkness of estrangement amidst the peoples and kindreds of the world may give way to the Light of Unity. Should other peoples and nations be unfaithful to you show your fidelity unto them, should they be unjust toward you show justice towards them, should they keep aloof from you attract them to yourselves, should they show their enmity be friendly towards them, should they poison your lives, sweeten their souls, should they inflict a wound upon you, be a salve to their sores. Such are the attributes of the sincere! Such are the attributes of the truthful." [39]

The quotation below helps us to understand how an awareness of the oneness of humanity affects social relations:

"I hope that each one of you will become just, and direct your thoughts towards the unity of mankind; that you will never harm your neighbors nor speak ill of anyone; that you will respect the rights of all men, and be more concerned for the interests of others than for your own." [40]

As for access to education, the following passage addresses this issue:

"Bahá'u'lláh has announced that inasmuch as ignorance and lack of education are barriers of separation among mankind, all must receive training and instruction. Through this provision the lack of mutual understanding will be remedied and the unity of mankind furthered and advanced. Universal education is a universal law." [41]

Regarding the administration of justice, we read the following:

> **"Divine civilization, however, so traineth every member of society that no one, with the exception of a negligible few, will undertake to commit a crime. There is thus a great difference between the prevention of crime through measures that are violent and retaliatory, and so training the people, and enlightening them, and spiritualizing them, that without any fear of punishment or vengeance to come, they will shun all criminal acts. They will, indeed, look upon the very commission of a crime as a great disgrace and in itself the harshest of punishments."** [42]

Having reflected on the above passages, you may wish to review the statements you wrote and consider whether you would like to modify any of them.

# SECTION 16

We have talked about a twofold moral purpose that impels individuals to take charge of their own spiritual and intellectual growth and contribute to the welfare of society. We have seen how this sense of purpose, so necessary for young people today, is strengthened by an understanding of the nature and the magnitude of the transformation in the individual and in society envisioned in the writings. What we also need to realize is that these two processes of change are intimately linked. Developing one's potential and working for the welfare of society cannot be separated, for a person's moral standards and conduct shape his or her environment and are, in turn, molded by the structure of society. A letter written on behalf of the Guardian states:

> **"We cannot segregate the human heart from the environment outside us and say that once one of these is reformed everything will be improved. Man is organic with the world. His inner life molds the environment and is itself also deeply affected by it. The one acts upon the other and every abiding change in the life of man is the result of these mutual reactions."** [43]

On the basis of the above quotation, decide whether the following statements are true or false:

a. The individual will be transformed only when society has been fully reformed.     T ☐   F ☐

b. Society's ills will completely vanish only when its individual members have become spiritual.     T ☐   F ☐

c. When just laws are enacted, society will be free from oppression, regardless of the way individuals may behave.     T ☐   F ☐

d. Society will be free from oppression when every individual strives to be just.     T ☐   F ☐

e.  All members of a society can be just even if the legal system operating in it is unjust.    T ☐ F ☐

f.  Once everyone becomes spiritual, the problems of society will be solved.    T ☐ F ☐

g.  An individual's conduct influences the social environment.    T ☐ F ☐

h.  A just society will be the result of efforts to create just structures and to educate individuals to be fair-minded and truth-seeking.    T ☐ F ☐

i.  No one can escape the effects of his or her social environment.    T ☐ F ☐

j.  Human beings, aided by their spiritual powers, can resist the negative effects of the social environment.    T ☐ F ☐

k.  Prejudice will disappear once everyone acknowledges the oneness of humanity.    T ☐ F ☐

l.  Prejudice will disappear only when society eradicates every trace of discrimination in its laws and institutions.    T ☐ F ☐

m.  Every form of prejudice can be abolished through the enactment of just laws and the training of souls to investigate reality and associate with everyone in love and fellowship.    T ☐ F ☐

n.  When everyone believes that humanity is one, we will have unity.    T ☐ F ☐

o.  The establishment of unity in the world requires the transformation of the individual and of the structure of society.    T ☐ F ☐

# SECTION 17

The ideas presented in the last section bring us back to the question of service, for it is in the field of service that we develop our potential and effect change in society. That participating in a process of social transformation implies a life dedicated to service needs little elaboration. What may require more thought, however, is the relationship between service and the intellectual and spiritual growth of the individual. Below is a list of activities. Many spiritual qualities need to come together in performing each one and in ensuring its effectiveness. For the purpose of this specific exercise, choose one or two qualities and attitudes that seem particularly relevant to each activity and try to describe how they contribute to the capacity of the individual to carry it out.

a. Holding a regular devotional meeting in a neighborhood or village: _____

_____

_____

b. Paying visits to friends and neighbors in order to discuss the Faith and reinforce ties of fellowship: _____

_____

_____

c. Conducting regular classes for the spiritual education of the young in a village or neighborhood: _____

_____

_____

d. Assisting a junior youth group as an animator over an extended period: _____

_____

_____

e. Teaching the Cause as part of a personal plan: _____

_____

_____

f. Teaching the Cause as part of a collective effort: _____

_____

_____

g. Acting as a tutor of a study circle, helping individuals not only to complete each course but also to implement its practical component: _____

_____

_____

The exercise above has helped us to think about how spiritual qualities and attitudes contribute to the capacity of an individual to carry out acts of service. But it is equally true that, in rendering service, one is able to develop and strengthen such qualities. Below are a few spiritual qualities that we are all striving to acquire. For each group, choose one of the activities above and describe in what ways you think it can contribute to the development of the qualities in the one who performs it.

a. Truthfulness, trustworthiness, and justice: _____

_____

_____

_____

_____

b. Forbearance and kindliness: _____

_____

_____

_____

_____

c. Sanctity, sincerity, and radiance: _____

_____

_____

_____

_____

d. Courage, trust, confidence, and humility: _____

_____

_____

_____

_____

e. Resignation and submissiveness to the Will of God: _____

_____

_____

_____

_____

# SECTION 18

Service is an all-embracing theme that touches every facet of our lives. When we are animated by a spirit of selfless service, every interaction we have, every action we take—in our professional lives, in our dealings with others, as members of our communities—is influenced by it. Yet, no matter what services we render, we remain ever conscious of the fact that there is a structured plan for the propagation of Bahá'u'lláh's message to the peoples of the world, a message which proclaims the oneness of humanity, calls for its unification, and provides laws and principles, spiritual and social teachings, that alone can establish a pattern for future society radically different from any seen in the past. Delineated by 'Abdu'l-Bahá Himself, this plan seeks nothing less than the spiritual regeneration of the world, and as it steadily unfolds through distinct stages, and more and more people participate in its execution, "a visible alternative to society's familiar strife is emerging." To it—the Divine Plan—should we dedicate ourselves. To it does the Guardian refer as "the mightiest Plan ever generated through the creative power of the Most Great Name". It is "forging ahead," he tells us,

". . . gaining momentum with every passing day, tearing down barriers in all climes and amidst divers peoples and races, widening irresistibly the scope of its beneficent operations, and revealing ever more compelling signs of its inherent strength as it marches towards the spiritual conquest of the entire planet." [44]

Through the Divine Plan, the spirit of Bahá'u'lláh's Revelation will become infused in all parts of the world, transforming individual and collective lives. Shoghi Effendi affirms moreover, that the

". . . final and crowning stage in the evolution of the plan wrought by God Himself for humanity will, in turn, prove to be the signal for the birth of a world civilization, incomparable in its range, its character and potency, in the history of mankind—a civilization which posterity will, with one voice, acclaim as the fairest fruit of the Golden Age of the Dispensation of Bahá'u'lláh . . ." [45]

In words such as the following does he appeal to the friends to contribute their share to the progress of the Plan:

"All must participate, however humble their origin, however limited their experience, however restricted their means, however deficient their education, however pressing their cares and preoccupations, however unfavorable the environment in which they live." [46]

And again:

"The field is indeed so immense, the period so critical, the Cause so great, the workers so few, the time so short, the privilege so priceless, that no follower of the Faith of Bahá'u'lláh, worthy to bear His name, can afford a moment's hesitation." [47]

Each stage in the unfoldment of the Divine Plan is marked by one of the global Plans launched by the Head of the Faith. Every Plan has certain requirements, and we know that the current series of Plans defines a framework for action which makes it possible for "an expanding nucleus of individuals" at the local level to generate the movement of a population "towards the goal of a new World Order". In this light, a message written by the Universal House of Justice to the participants in a series of youth conferences held throughout the world in 2013 explains:

"After many a decade, the world-embracing labors of this far-flung community to obtain a more adequate understanding of the Revelation of Bahá'u'lláh and to apply the principles it enshrines have culminated in the emergence of a potent framework for action, refined through experience. You are fortunate to be familiar with its methods and approaches now so well established. Through perseverance in their implementation, many of you will already have seen for yourselves signs of the society-building power of the divine teachings. At the conference you attend, you are being invited to consider the contribution that can be made by any young person who wishes to answer Bahá'u'lláh's summons and help to release that power." [48]

And the same message notes further:

> "The possibilities presented by collective action are especially evident in the work of community building, a process that is gaining momentum in many a cluster and in neighborhoods and villages throughout the world that have become centers of intense activity. Youth are often at the forefront of the work in these settings—not only Bahá'í youth, but those of like mind who can see the positive effects of what the Bahá'ís have initiated and grasp the underlying vision of unity and spiritual transformation. In such places, the imperative to share the Revelation of Bahá'u'lláh with receptive hearts and explore the implications of His message for today's world is keenly felt. When so much of society invites passivity and apathy or, worse still, encourages behavior harmful to oneself and others, a conspicuous contrast is offered by those who are enhancing the capacity of a population to cultivate and sustain a spiritually enriching pattern of community life." [49]

And with these words does the House of Justice, in another message, encourage Bahá'í youth and those who wish to join them:

> "To every generation of young believers comes an opportunity to make a contribution to the fortunes of humanity, unique to their time of life. For the present generation, the moment has come to reflect, to commit, to steel themselves for a life of service from which blessing will flow in abundance. In our prayers at the Sacred Threshold, we entreat the Ancient Beauty that, from out a distracted and bewildered humanity, He may distil pure souls endowed with clear sight: youth whose integrity and uprightness are not undermined by dwelling on the faults of others and who are not immobilized by any shortcomings of their own; youth who will look to the Master and 'bring those who have been excluded into the circle of intimate friends'; youth whose consciousness of the failings of society impels them to work for its transformation, not to distance themselves from it; youth who, whatever the cost, will refuse to pass by inequity in its many incarnations and will labor, instead, that 'the light of justice may shed its radiance upon the whole world.'" [50]

The above quotations can leave little doubt in your mind of the imperative need for young people to move to the front ranks of those serving the Divine Plan. To end this section, it would be helpful for you to reflect on the following message written by the Universal House of Justice to a series of youth gatherings held in 2000 across Latin America:

> "As this generation of youth assumes the responsibilities of conducting the affairs of society, it will encounter a landscape of bewildering contrast. On the one hand, the region can justly boast brilliant achievements in the intellectual, technological and economic spheres. On the other, it has failed to reduce widespread poverty or to avoid a rising sea of violence that threatens to submerge its peoples. Why—and the question needs to be asked plainly—has this society been impotent, despite its great wealth, to remove the injustices that are tearing its fiber apart?

**"The answer to this question, as amply evidenced by decades of contentious history, cannot be found in political passion, conflicting expressions of class interest, or technical recipes. What is called for is a spiritual revival, as a prerequisite to the successful application of political, economic and technological instruments. But there is a need for a catalyst. Be assured that, in spite of your small numbers, you are the channels through which such a catalyst can be provided." [51]**

1.  The message asks why a society with such intellectual, technological, and economic wealth has been unable to remove the injustices tearing it apart, indicating that the answer is not to be found in political passion, conflicting expressions of class interest, or technical recipes. Think of the society in which you live and give an example of each of the following:

    a.  A political passion that characterizes the society: _____

    _____

    _____

    _____

    b.  Some of the conflicting expressions of class interest in the society: _____

    _____

    _____

    _____

    c.  A technical recipe that the society has followed: _____

    _____

    _____

    _____

2.  What, according to the Universal House of Justice, is a prerequisite to the successful application of political, economic, and technological instruments in efforts to eliminate social ills? _____

    _____

3.  What does the House of Justice tell us is needed to bring about the spiritual revival of society? _____

    _____

4.  Who does the House of Justice say constitutes a channel through which Bahá'u'lláh's message to humanity can be provided? _____

    _____

Now, with the above thoughts in mind, discuss with your friends studying this course how participation in the execution of the Divine Plan enables young people to act as channels for the spiritual revival of society.

# SECTION 19

No doubt the discussion at the end of the last section caused you to think further about the essential role young people are to play in the onward march of the Cause. In the passage below from *God Passes By,* Shoghi Effendi presents a picture of the early champions of the Faith, whose heroic deeds are to inspire humanity throughout the ages. Given that many of them were young people themselves, we would do well to reflect here on the words the Guardian employed to describe their outstanding qualities. Before doing so, you may find it useful to read through the following glossary:

| | |
|---|---|
| Meteor-like: | Like a meteor; a luminous trail that appears in the sky and moves quickly across |
| Traverse: | Travel across |
| Somber: | Dark and gloomy |
| Satellite: | A celestial body orbiting another of a larger size |
| Galaxy: | A very large group of stars |
| Irradiate: | Send out rays of light |
| Incandescent: | Glowing with intense heat; strikingly bright |
| Nascent: | Having recently come into existence |
| Contest: | A struggle for victory |
| Trail-breakers: | Pioneers |
| Intrigue: | Secret scheme |
| Depravity: | Corruption; wickedness |
| Sweeping: | Of wide range; overwhelming |
| Piety: | Reverence for God and devotion to religious duty |
| Fervor: | Intensity of feeling |
| Leonine: | Like a lion |
| Abnegation: | Renouncing; giving up |
| Resolve: | Strong purpose |
| Granite-like: | Unyielding in firmness and endurance |
| Stupendous: | Of amazing greatness |
| Veneration: | Respect and awe |
| Disconcerting: | Bewildering; perplexing |

The Guardian writes:

> **"We behold, as we survey the episodes of this first act of a sublime drama, the figure of its Master Hero, the Báb, arise meteor-like above the horizon of <u>Sh</u>íráz, traverse the somber sky of Persia from south to north, decline with tragic swiftness, and perish in a blaze of glory. We see His satellites, a galaxy of God-intoxicated heroes, mount above that same horizon, irradiate that same incandescent light, burn themselves out with that self-same swiftness, and**

**impart in their turn an added impetus to the steadily gathering momentum
of God's nascent Faith. . . .**

"**The heroes whose deeds shine upon the record of this fierce spiritual contest,
involving at once people, clergy, monarch and government, were the Báb's
chosen disciples, the Letters of the Living, and their companions, the trail-
breakers of the New Day, who to so much intrigue, ignorance, depravity,
cruelty, superstition and cowardice opposed a spirit exalted, unquenchable
and awe-inspiring, a knowledge surprisingly profound, an eloquence sweeping
in its force, a piety unexcelled in fervor, a courage leonine in its fierceness,
a self-abnegation saintly in its purity, a resolve granite-like in its firmness, a
vision stupendous in its range, a veneration for the Prophet and His Imáms
disconcerting to their adversaries, a power of persuasion alarming to their
antagonists, a standard of faith and a code of conduct that challenged and
revolutionized the lives of their countrymen.**" [52]

1.  Complete the following sentences:

    a.  The Letters of the Living and their companions were engaged in a _____
        contest.

    b.  This contest involved at once _____ , _____ , _____
        and _____ .

    c.  The early heroes of the Faith opposed intrigue, ignorance, depravity, cruelty,
        superstition and cowardice with

        — a spirit _____ , _____ and _____

        _____ ,

        — a knowledge _____ ,

        — an eloquence _____ ,

        — a piety _____ ,

        — a courage _____ ,

        — a self-abnegation _____ ,

        — a resolve _____ ,

        — a vision _____ ,

        — a veneration for the Prophet and His Imáms _____

        _____ ,

        — a power of persuasion _____ ,

        — a standard of faith and a code of conduct that _____

        _____

        _____ .

2.  For what purpose did the early heroes of the Faith enter into the spiritual contest described by the Guardian in the passage above? _____

_____

_____

_____

3.  Are the Bahá'í youth of the present age, like their predecessors, engaged in a spiritual contest? _____

4.  How does their contest resemble that of the early heroes of the Faith? _____

_____

_____

_____

5.  How can the Bahá'í youth of today ensure that, like their brothers and sisters in the Heroic Age of the Faith, they are able to succeed in the spiritual contest in which they are engaged? _____

_____

_____

_____

Before moving onto the next section, you may wish to reflect on the following passage from a message written by the Universal House of Justice:

> **"When the exalted figure of the Báb, aged just twenty-five, arose to deliver His revolutionizing message to the world, many among those who accepted and spread His teachings were young, even younger than the Báb Himself. Their heroism, immortalized in all its dazzling intensity in *The Dawn-Breakers*, will illumine the annals of human history for centuries to come. Thus began a pattern in which every generation of youth, drawing inspiration from the same divine impulse to cast the world anew, has seized the opportunity to contribute to the latest stage in the unfolding process that is to transform the life of humankind. It is a pattern that has suffered no interruption from the time of the Báb to this present hour."** [53]

## SECTION 20

Through successive cycles of crisis and victory, youth of every generation have followed the trail blazed by the dawn-breakers and have remained in the forefront of Bahá'í activity, laboring to bring Bahá'u'lláh's message to humanity. The Universal House of Justice writes:

> **"From the very beginning of the Bahá'í Era, youth have played a vital part in the promulgation of God's Revelation. The Báb Himself was but twenty-five years old when He declared His Mission, while many of the Letters of the**

Living were even younger. The Master, as a very young man, was called upon to shoulder heavy responsibilities in the service of His Father in Iraq and Turkey, and His brother, the Purest Branch, yielded up his life to God in the Most Great Prison at the age of twenty-two that the servants of God might 'be quickened, and all that dwell on earth be united.' Shoghi Effendi was a student at Oxford when called to the throne of his guardianship, and many of the Knights of Bahá'u'lláh, who won imperishable fame during the Ten Year Crusade, were young people." [54]

In a message written in 1984, the House of Justice pays tribute to the heroes of a more recent past:

"Consider, for example, the instances in Shíráz last summer of the six young women, their ages ranging from 18 to 25 years, whose lives were snuffed out by the hangman's noose. All faced attempted inducements to recant their faith; all refused to deny their Beloved. Look also at the accounts of the astounding fortitude shown over and over again by children and youth who were subjected to the interrogations and abuses of teachers and mullahs and were expelled from school for upholding their beliefs. It, moreover, bears noting that under the restrictions so cruelly imposed on their community, the youth rendered signal services, placing their energies at the disposal of Bahá'í institutions throughout the country. No splendor of speech could give more fitting testimony to their spiritual commitment and fidelity than these pure acts of selflessness and devotion. In virtually no other place on earth is so great a price for faith required of the Bahá'ís. Nor could there be found more willing, more radiant bearers of the cup of sacrifice than the valiant Bahá'í youth of Iran. Might it, then, not be reasonably expected that you, the youth and young adults living at such an extraordinary time, witnessing such stirring examples of the valor of your Iranian fellows, and exercising such freedom of movement, would sally forth, 'unrestrained as the wind,' into the field of Bahá'í action?" [55]

Opportunities to reflect on significant events in the lives of heroic souls around the world can help each generation of youth acquire a sense of mission. Close bonds are formed with these outstanding figures in childhood through stories narrated in weekly children's classes and at home, but a more deliberate effort is required to address this need between the ages of twelve to fifteen and, of course, throughout the entire period of youth. Carefully selected examples, some dramatic and others less so, can demonstrate such qualities as courage, determination, zeal, and selflessness that young people must strive to emulate.

1.  Identify either from the early history of the Faith or from more recent times a few episodes upon which you feel youth should reflect. _____

    _____

    _____

    _____

2.  Give your reason for selecting these particular episodes. _____

    _____

    _____

    _____

# SECTION 21

Even from the small sampling of passages quoted above, it is possible to see that the lives of the early champions of the Faith and the heroic souls that followed them were distinguished by a sense of purpose. It is equally evident that they each must have possessed an understanding of the significance of the historical moment in which they were living, as well as a vision of the magnitude of the change which humanity was being called upon to make. That this sense of purpose found expression in a life dedicated to the diffusion of the Divine message is also clear. Yet, as we reflect on the heroic deeds they performed and on the ultimate sacrifice many of them made, we cannot believe that these attributes alone distinguished such sanctified beings. What was it that characterized their lives most? What passion possessed them, and what drove them to reach such heights of selfless service? Was it not the love of God that burned so brightly in their hearts? Were they not intoxicated by the beauty of their Beloved? Can we ever hope to contribute to the spiritual empowerment of the next generation of youth if we do not foster in them an attraction to beauty, if we do not nurture their innate desire to partake of the soft-flowing streams of true knowledge, if we do not help them develop an intimate relationship with their Creator? Let us end this unit by immersing ourselves in the following words:

> **"For when the true lover and devoted friend reacheth to the presence of the Beloved, the sparkling beauty of the Loved One and the fire of the lover's heart will kindle a blaze and burn away all veils and wrappings. Yea, all he hath, from heart to skin, will be set aflame, so that nothing will remain save the Friend."** [56]

> **"O Friends! Abandon not the everlasting beauty for a beauty that must die, and set not your affections on this mortal world of dust."** [57]

> **"Know thou that he is truly learned who hath acknowledged My Revelation, and drunk from the Ocean of My knowledge, and soared in the atmosphere of My love, and cast away all else besides Me, and taken firm hold on that which hath been sent down from the Kingdom of My wondrous utterance. He, verily, is even as an eye unto mankind, and as the spirit of life unto the body of all creation. Glorified be the All-Merciful Who hath enlightened him, and caused him to arise and serve His great and mighty Cause. Verily, such a man is blessed by the Concourse on high, and by them who dwell within the Tabernacle of Grandeur, who have quaffed My sealed Wine in My Name, the Omnipotent, the All-Powerful."** [58]

> **"O army of God! Whensoever ye behold a person whose entire attention is directed toward the Cause of God; whose only aim is this, to make the Word of God to take effect; who, day and night, with pure intent, is rendering service to the Cause; from whose behavior not the slightest trace of egotism or private motives is discerned—who, rather, wandereth distracted in the wilderness of the love of God, and drinketh only from the cup of the knowledge of God, and is utterly engrossed in spreading the sweet savors of God, and is enamored of the holy verses of the Kingdom of God—know ye for a certainty that this individual will be supported and reinforced by heaven; that like unto the morning star, he will forever gleam brightly out of the skies of eternal grace. But if he show the slightest taint of selfish desires and self love, his efforts will lead to nothing and he will be destroyed and left hopeless at the last."** [59]

"Know thou verily, the hand of divine Providence hath attracted thee to the Throne of the Kingdom, and the divine glad-tidings hath caused such joy and happiness in thee, that thou hast removed the covering and lifted the veiling from the Countenance of the Divine Beauty, beheld the Brilliant Face through thine insight, and became cognizant of the mysteries of purity and sanctity in this divine Cause!

"Now, with a heart overflowing with the love of God, supplicate to God with all joy, and thank thou God for this guidance and this high gift. And know thou, that verily, the vanguards of the gifts of thy Lord shall overtake thee from all sides when thy feet become firm in the Path." [60]

"O my God! O my God! This, Thy servant, hath advanced towards Thee, is passionately wandering in the desert of Thy love, walking in the path of Thy service, anticipating Thy favors, hoping for Thy bounty, relying upon Thy kingdom, and intoxicated by the wine of Thy gift. O my God! Increase the fervor of his affection for Thee, the constancy of his praise of Thee, and the ardor of his love for Thee.

"Verily, Thou art the Most Generous, the Lord of grace abounding. There is no other God but Thee, the Forgiving, the Merciful." [61]

# REFERENCES

1.  'Abdu'l-Bahá, in *Bahá'í Prayers and Tablets for the Young* (Wilmette: Bahá'í Publishing Trust, 1978), p. 30.

2.  'Abdu'l-Bahá, in *Bahá'í Prayers: A Selection of Prayers Revealed by Bahá'u'lláh, the Báb, and 'Abdu'l-Bahá* (Wilmette: Bahá'í Publishing Trust, 2002, 2011 printing), pp. 252–53.

3.  *Selections from the Writings of 'Abdu'l-Bahá* (Wilmette: Bahá'í Publishing Trust, 1997, 2009 printing), no. 225, p. 298.

4.  'Abdu'l-Bahá, in *Bahá'í Prayers,* p. 254.

5.  Bahá'u'lláh, in "Extracts Relating to the Subject of Youth", published in *The Compilation of Compilations* (Maryborough: Bahá'í Publications Australia, 1991), vol. 2, p. 415.

6.  From a letter dated 1 September 1933 written on behalf of Shoghi Effendi to an individual believer, published in *Youth: Channels for Change* (Riviera Beach: Palabra Publications, 2001), p. 5.

7.  From a message dated 25 May 1975 written by the Universal House of Justice to all National Spiritual Assemblies, published in *Messages from the Universal House of Justice, 1963–1986: The Third Epoch of the Formative Age* (Wilmette: Bahá'í Publishing Trust, 1996), no. 162, p. 310.

8.  From a letter dated 8 August 1957 written on behalf of Shoghi Effendi to a group of Bahá'í youth, published in *Youth*, p. 3.

9.  From a letter dated 28 December 1925 written on behalf of Shoghi Effendi to a group of Bahá'í youth, in ibid., p. 36.

10. From a message dated 10 June 1966 written by the Universal House of Justice to the Bahá'í youth in every land, published in *Messages from the Universal House of Justice, 1963–1986,* no. 37, p. 92.

11. From an unpublished letter dated 23 February 1995 written on behalf of the Universal House of Justice to selected National Spiritual Assemblies.

12. From an unpublished letter dated 23 April 2013 written on behalf of the Universal House of Justice to a National Spiritual Assembly.

13. From an unpublished letter dated 19 April 2013 written on behalf of the Universal House of Justice to a small group of individual believers.

14. From a message dated 12 December 2011 written by the Universal House of Justice to all National Spiritual Assemblies, published in *The Five Year Plan, 2011–2016: Messages of the Universal House of Justice* (West Palm Beach: Palabra Publications, 2013), p. 81.

15. *Gleanings from the Writings of Bahá'u'lláh* (Wilmette: Bahá'í Publishing, 2005), no. 137, p. 338.

16. From a letter dated 8 December 1923 written by Shoghi Effendi to a Bahá'í community, published in *Trustworthiness: A Compilation of Extracts from the Bahá'í Writings,* compiled by the Research Department of the Universal House of Justice (London: Bahá'í Publishing Trust, 1987), p. 19.

17. *'Abdu'l-Bahá in London: Addresses and Notes of Conversations* (London: Bahá'í Publishing Trust, 1982), p. 66.

18. *Gleanings from the Writings of Bahá'u'lláh,* no. 29, p. 78.

19. Bahá'u'lláh, in *Trustworthiness,* p. 5.

20. 'Abdu'l-Bahá, *The Secret of Divine Civilization* (Wilmette: Bahá'í Publishing, 2007), p. 5.

21. Ibid., p. 6.

22. *Gleanings from the Writings of Bahá'u'lláh,* no. 43, p. 105.

23. Ibid., no. 126, p. 306.

24. Bahá'u'lláh, cited by Shoghi Effendi, *The Advent of Divine Justice* (Wilmette: Bahá'í Publishing Trust, 2006), p. 47.

25. *Gleanings from the Writings of Baha'u'lláh,* no. 60, p. 133.

26. Bahá'u'lláh, cited by Shoghi Effendi, *The Advent of Divine Justice,* p. 34.

27. Ibid., pp. 34–35.

28. *Tablets of Abdul-Baha Abbas* (New York: Bahá'í Publishing Committee, 1915, 1940 printing), vol. 2, p. 436. (authorized translation)

29. *Gleanings from the Writings of Bahá'u'lláh,* no. 143, p. 354.

30. Ibid., no. 70, p. 154.

31. 'Abdu'l-Bahá, *Some Answered Questions* (Wilmette: Bahá'í Publishing Trust, 1984, 2009 printing), p. 39.

32. *The Promulgation of Universal Peace: Talks Delivered by 'Abdu'l-Bahá during His Visit to the United States and Canada in 1912* (Wilmette: Bahá'í Publishing, 2012), p. 618.

33. Ibid., p. 405.

34. Bahá'u'lláh, *The Hidden Words* (Wilmette: Bahá'í Publishing Trust, 2003), Persian no. 6, p. 24.

35.  *Will and Testament of 'Abdu'l-Bahá* (Wilmette: Bahá'í Publishing Trust, 1944, 2002 printing), p. 13.

36.  *The Hidden Words,* Persian no. 49, p. 39.

37.  *Selections from the Writings of 'Abdu'l-Bahá,* no. 10, p. 30.

38.  From the address of the Báb to the Letters of the Living, in *The Dawn-Breakers: Nabíl's Narrative of the Early Days of the Bahá'í Revelation* (Wilmette: Bahá'í Publishing Trust, 1932, 1999 printing), p. 93.

39.  *Will and Testament of 'Abdu'l-Bahá,* p. 14.

40.  *Paris Talks: Addresses Given by 'Abdu'l-Bahá in 1911* (Wilmette: Bahá'í Publishing, 2011), pp. 199–200.

41.  *The Promulgation of Universal Peace*, p. 417.

42.  *Selections from the Writings of 'Abdu'l-Bahá*, no. 105, p. 140.

43.  From a letter dated 17 February 1933 written on behalf of Shoghi Effendi to an individual believer, published in *Conservation of the Earth's Resources,* compiled by the Research Department of the Universal House of Justice (London: Bahá'í Publishing Trust, 1990), p. 15.

44.  From a message dated March 1955 written by Shoghi Effendi, published in *Messages to the Bahá'í World, 1950–1957* (Wilmette: Bahá'í Publishing Trust, 1971, 1999 printing), p. 76.

45.  From a letter dated 4 May 1953 written by Shoghi Effendi, in ibid., p. 155.

46.  *The Advent of Divine Justice*, p. 68.

47.  Ibid., p. 70.

48.  From a message dated 1 July 2013 written by the Universal House of Justice to the participants in the forthcoming 114 youth conferences throughout the world, published in *The Five Year Plan, 2011–2016*, pp. 105–6.

49.  Ibid., pp. 107–8.

50.  From a message dated 8 February 2013 written by the Universal House of Justice to the Bahá'ís of the world, in ibid., pp. 93–94.

51.  From a message dated 8 January 2000 written by the Universal House of Justice to the friends gathered at the youth congress in Paraguay, published in *Turning Point: Selected Messages of the Universal House of Justice and Supplementary Material, 1996–2006* (West Palm Beach: Palabra Publications, 2006), pp. 123–24.

52.  Shoghi Effendi, *God Passes By* (Wilmette: Bahá'í Publishing Trust, 1974, 2010 printing), pp. 4–6.

53. From a message dated 1 July 2013 written by the Universal House of Justice to the participants in the forthcoming 114 youth conferences throughout the world, published in *The Five Year Plan, 2011–2016*, p. 105.

54. From a message dated 10 June 1966 written by the Universal House of Justice to the Bahá'í youth in every land, published in *Messages from the Universal House of Justice, 1963–1986*, no. 37, p. 92.

55. From a message dated 3 January 1984 written by the Universal House of Justice to the Bahá'í youth of the world, in ibid., no. 386, p. 616.

56. Bahá'u'lláh, *The Seven Valleys and The Four Valleys* (Wilmette: Bahá'í Publishing Trust, 1991, 2004 printing), p. 36.

57. *The Hidden Words,* Persian no. 14, p. 26.

58. *Tablets of Bahá'u'lláh Revealed after the Kitáb-i-Aqdas* (Wilmette: Bahá'í Publishing Trust, 1988, 2005 printing), pp. 207–8.

59. *Selections from the Writings of 'Abdu'l-Bahá,* no. 35, pp. 76–77.

60. *Tablets of Abdul-Baha Abbas* (New York: Bahá'í Publishing Committee, 1909, 1930 printing), vol. 1, p. 182.

61. 'Abdu'l-Bahá, in *Bahá'í Prayers,* p. 176.

# An Age of Promise

## Purpose

To explore the immense potentialities
of young people between the ages of twelve and fifteen
and to appreciate the significance of providing them
with an environment conducive to their spiritual empowerment.

## Practice

To converse with a few junior youth
in one's village, town, or neighborhood
about their views on life and
their aspirations for the future.

# SECTION 1

In the previous unit, we discussed some of the characteristics that are to distinguish youth. The purpose of this unit is to reflect on the immense potentialities of junior youth and the forces that shape their lives. The concepts you will be examining here have been progressively consolidated through decades of experience. The special needs of those between the ages of twelve and fifteen have long been recognized by the Bahá'í community. From the early attempts to educate members of this age group and subsequent efforts to learn how to unlock their capacity and to channel their surging energies, the junior youth spiritual empowerment program we are exploring in this book gradually emerged. You may be familiar with the program, having participated in it yourself when you were younger or having worked alongside one of your friends carrying it out in your village or neighborhood. The material you are studying now is intended to help you dedicate three years initially, but perhaps more, to this meritorious field of service, enabling you to assist several members of an age group so full of promise in navigating a crucial stage of their lives.

Regarding the junior youth spiritual empowerment program, the Universal House of Justice writes:

> **"The rapid spread of the program for the spiritual empowerment of junior youth is yet another expression of cultural advance in the Bahá'í community. While global trends project an image of this age group as problematic, lost in the throes of tumultuous physical and emotional change, unresponsive and self-consumed, the Bahá'í community—in the language it employs and the approaches it adopts—is moving decidedly in the opposite direction, seeing in junior youth instead altruism, an acute sense of justice, eagerness to learn about the universe and a desire to contribute to the construction of a better world. Account after account, in which junior youth in countries all over the planet give voice to their thoughts as participants in the program, testifies to the validity of this vision. There is every indication that the program engages their expanding consciousness in an exploration of reality that helps them to analyze the constructive and destructive forces operating in society and to recognize the influence these forces exert on their thoughts and actions, sharpening their spiritual perception, enhancing their powers of expression and reinforcing moral structures that will serve them throughout their lives. At an age when burgeoning intellectual, spiritual and physical powers become accessible to them, they are being given the tools needed to combat the forces that would rob them of their true identity as noble beings and to work for the common good."** [1]

Many of the concepts and ideas mentioned by the House of Justice in the above passage are the very focus of this unit of study, and as you move through it, they will become further clarified in your mind. For now, you may wish to answer the following questions:

1.  Why do young people between the ages of twelve and fifteen represent such a special group? _____

    _____

    _____

2.  What do you think are some of the distinctive needs of this younger generation?

_____

_____

_____

_____

3.  What does the Universal House of Justice indicate are some of the features of the junior youth spiritual empowerment program? _____

_____

_____

_____

_____

4.  What motivates you to enter this particular area of service? _____

_____

_____

_____

_____


# SECTION 2

Bahá'u'lláh tells us that an individual reaches the beginning of maturity at the age of fifteen, when laws such as those dealing with obligatory prayer and fasting become binding. Viewed from this perspective, the years immediately before that age take on special significance. It is during those few years that the transition from childhood to the period of youth occurs. The sudden and rapid changes generally associated with this transition—physical, intellectual, and emotional—influence behavior in a number of ways.

By the age of twelve, signs of transition have begun to appear. Many youngsters will grow more physically over the next three to four years than at any other stage of their lives. They will gain in height and body mass and will experience hormonal changes. Boys will develop deep voices, and girls will begin to form the physique of young women. Both will go through puberty, acquiring the physical ability to beget children.

The physical and emotional changes that a person experiences during this period are interrelated. Excitement over the emergence of new powers and an eagerness to wield them are accompanied by awkwardness, sensitivity, and feelings of anxiety. These emotions may give rise to contradictory behavior. One may seem shy, yet on occasion be quite sociable; may express the desire to be left alone, yet equally welcome attention; may have incredible courage in some situations and be rather fearful in others. Growing concern with one's own talents and abilities gradually manifests itself, as does an increased sense of awareness of one's place in the world, particularly in the context of one's relationship with both peers and adults. The way others see one's appearance and react to one's ideas takes on importance.

Further, during the few years before we reach the age of fifteen, fundamental concepts about individual and collective life are formulated in our minds. Our power of analysis becomes stronger, and we may begin to question much of what we have been taught and to see contradictions in the world around us that had previously gone unnoticed. We are not as willing as before to follow automatically the standards set by adults. One is ever seeking answers to questions, often philosophical in nature, during this time of transition, and a new consciousness rapidly develops.

If young people are to be assisted in applying fruitfully their emerging powers, it is essential to avoid treating them in ways that tend to, on the one hand, prolong their childhood and, on the other, encourage them to imitate a version of adulthood superficial in so many of its aspects—a trend that, unfortunately, is taking root in more and more societies. 'Abdu'l-Bahá indicates:

> **"After a time he enters the period of youth, in which his former conditions and needs are superseded by new requirements applicable to the advance in his degree. His faculties of observation are broadened and deepened; his intelligent capacities are trained and awakened; the limitations and environment of childhood no longer restrict his energies and accomplishments."** [2]

To enhance your understanding of the differences between the years of childhood and the period of youth, discuss the following questions in your group:

1.    What does it mean for faculties of observation to broaden and deepen? Can you illustrate your comments with a few examples? _____

    _____

    _____

    _____

    _____

2.    How do the intellectual capacities of a junior youth differ from those of a child?

    _____

    _____

    _____

    _____

3.    What are some of the limitations of childhood that no longer restrict the energies of a junior youth? _____

    _____

    _____

    _____

# SECTION 3

Every individual should receive the kind of education and nurturing in the years immediately before the age of fifteen that will allow the attributes inherent in the period of youth to emerge. The need for such an education becomes especially clear when it is recognized that, by the age of fifteen, many of the patterns of thought and conduct of an individual will have already been fixed. As 'Abdu'l-Bahá explains,

> **"it is extremely difficult to teach the individual and refine his character once puberty is passed. By then, as experience hath shown, even if every effort be exerted to modify some tendency of his, it all availeth nothing. He may, perhaps, improve somewhat today; but let a few days pass and he forgetteth, and turneth backward to his habitual condition and accustomed ways." [3]**

You are familiar with the term "adolescence", which is often used loosely in referring to young people anywhere from around the age of twelve to as old as eighteen. Sometimes the phrase "early adolescence" is used to identify those in the age range we generally call "junior youth". Here we are not overly particular in this respect and employ the terms "junior youth", "adolescence", and "early adolescence" interchangeably. To think about the importance of education during adolescence, decide whether the following statements are true or false:

a. Even if proper education is not received in childhood, appropriate nurturing during adolescence can help to correct any undesirable patterns of conduct established earlier.　　T ☐ F ☐

b. Only those individuals who have received spiritual and moral education in childhood are able to develop their full potential.　　T ☐ F ☐

c. Without proper attention and care during adolescence, an individual could go astray, even if throughout childhood he or she received moral and spiritual education.　　T ☐ F ☐

d. It is during adolescence that individuals begin to align their lives with forces that advance society or allow themselves to be carried away by forces of social disintegration.　　T ☐ F ☐


# SECTION 4

Rising awareness during adolescence can be directed towards one of two ends: towards submission to the Will of God and self-sacrificing service to humanity or towards captivity in the prison of self and passion. 'Abdu'l-Bahá makes clear:

> **"The individuality of each created thing is based upon divine wisdom, for in the creation of God there is no defect. However, personality has no element of permanence. It is a slightly changeable quality in man which can be turned in either direction. For if he acquire praiseworthy virtues, these strengthen**

the individuality of man and call forth his hidden forces; but if he acquire defects, the beauty and simplicity of the individuality will be lost to him and its God-given qualities will be stifled in the foul atmosphere of self." [4]

We live in an age when an aggressive materialistic culture is invading every facet of life. The exaggerated preoccupation with self that is woven into the fabric of this pervasive culture presents us with numerous challenges as we try to assist youth in developing their capacities, for even efforts that sincerely seek to help young people realize their potential and direct their energies towards the common good can suffer from the adverse influence of a worldview individualistic at its core. The problem is complex. Today's world system does deprive vast numbers of human beings of the fortitude required to lead purposeful lives; therefore, confidence in one's moral strength is an issue to be addressed. It crushes people's true identity; therefore, the realization of one's noble aspirations is a legitimate concern. It makes multitudes oblivious of the life of the soul; therefore, discovery of one's true potential deserves attention. Yet, programs that emphasize the "self" do not necessarily remedy the situation. What frequently happens is that, in the name of self-realization, self-discovery, and self-esteem, such programs romanticize the individual and bolster the ego. Our challenge is to nurture spiritual susceptibilities in the young, that their tender hearts may be stirred by attraction to the Most Great Beauty and turned towards the high ideals of selfless service to humanity. Our efforts to tend to the educational needs of this formative phase in their lives must prevent the insistent self from asserting itself. In order to explore the nature of this challenge, you are asked, in the next few sections, to reflect on some of the passages from the writings that refer to the self. First, however, you may find it useful to discuss in your group the meaning of the phrase "the insistent self asserting itself". How can one ensure that service does not become the arena in which the self gains ascendance?

# SECTION 5

The first set of quotations below is related to aspects of "individuality" that are pleasing to God and should be developed:

> "O My servants! Could ye apprehend with what wonders of My munificence and bounty I have willed to entrust your souls, ye would, of a truth, rid yourselves of attachment to all created things, and would gain a true knowledge of your own selves—a knowledge which is the same as the comprehension of Mine own Being. Ye would find yourselves independent of all else but Me, and would perceive, with your inner and outer eye, and as manifest as the revelation of My effulgent Name, the seas of My loving-kindness and bounty moving within you." [5]

> "Far, far from Thy glory be what mortal man can affirm of Thee, or attribute unto Thee, or the praise with which he can glorify Thee! Whatever duty Thou hast prescribed unto Thy servants of extolling to the utmost Thy majesty and glory is but a token of Thy grace unto them, that they may be enabled to ascend unto the station conferred upon their own inmost being, the station of the knowledge of their own selves." [6]

"The first Ṭaráz and the first effulgence which hath dawned from the horizon of the Mother Book is that man should know his own self and recognize that which leadeth unto loftiness or lowliness, glory or abasement, wealth or poverty." [7]

"O Son of Spirit! I created thee rich, why dost thou bring thyself down to poverty? Noble I made thee, wherewith dost thou abase thyself? Out of the essence of knowledge I gave thee being, why seekest thou enlightenment from anyone beside Me? Out of the clay of love I molded thee, how dost thou busy thyself with another? Turn thy sight unto thyself, that thou mayest find Me standing within thee, mighty, powerful and self-subsisting." [8]

Complete the following sentences on the basis of the above quotations:

a. When we apprehend with what wonders of His munificence and bounty God has willed to entrust our souls, we will _____ _____ , and will _____ _____ .

b. We will find ourselves _____ , and will perceive, with our inner and outer eye, _____ _____ _____ _____ .

c. Whatever duty has been prescribed unto us of extolling God's majesty and glory is but a token of His grace unto us, that we may be enabled to _____ _____ _____ _____ .

d. We should know our own selves and recognize that which leads unto _____ or _____ , _____ or _____ , _____ or _____ .

e. We have been created _____ , and been made _____ . Out of the essence of _____ God has given us being, and out of the clay of _____ He has _____ us. He asks us to turn our sights unto ourselves, that we may _____ _____ .

The above quotations all refer to our true self and the importance of understanding its nature. We should realize, of course, that knowledge of the nobility of our being does not lead to self-aggrandizement but to humility before God and His servants. Discuss in your group how knowledge of our true self assists us in our struggle against the ego.

# SECTION 6

The second set of quotations warns us of the consequences of indulging the self:

**"Every imperfect soul is self-centered and thinketh only of his own good."** [9]

**"But if he show the slightest taint of selfish desires and self-love, his efforts will lead to nothing and he will be destroyed and left hopeless at the last."** [10]

**"In particular thou wishest for deliverance from self-conceit. This quality, which is pride, hath been the ruin of many important people in the world. Should a person be possessed of all praiseworthy qualities yet be egotistical, then all those virtues and goodly characteristics will be obliterated, and ultimately converted into the worst of defects."** [11]

**"Despair, both here and hereafter, is all you will gain from self-indulgence; abomination and misery are all you will harvest from fanaticism, from believing the foolish and the mindless."** [12]

**"Today, all the peoples of the world are indulging in self-interest and exert the utmost effort and endeavor to promote their own material interests. They are worshipping themselves and not the divine reality, nor the world of mankind."** [13]

**"These tests, even as thou didst write, do but cleanse the spotting of self from off the mirror of the heart, till the Sun of Truth can cast its rays thereon; for there is no veil more obstructive than the self, and however tenuous that veil may be, at the last it will completely shut a person out, and deprive him of his portion of eternal grace."** [14]

**"Behold how the sun shines upon all creation, but only surfaces that are pure and polished can reflect its glory and light. The darkened soul has no portion of the revelation of the glorious effulgence of reality; and the soil of self, unable to take advantage of that light, does not produce growth."** [15]

**"How debased the soul which can find enjoyment in this darkness, occupied with itself, the captive of self and passion, wallowing in the mire of the material world!"** [16]

"Self-centeredness", "self-love", "self-worship", "self-conceit", "indulgence in self-interest", and "captivity of self and passion" give rise to that atmosphere which stifles the God-given attributes of our individuality. In light of the above passages, describe in a few sentences how preoccupation with self arrests spiritual growth and moral development and diminishes the effectiveness of service.

_____

_____

_____

_____

_____

_____

_____

_____

_____

_____

# SECTION 7

The third set of quotations represents a small sampling of the many counsels found in the writings on how to treat the insistent self:

> "Today the confirmations of the Kingdom of Abhá are with those who renounce themselves, forget their own opinions, cast aside personalities and are thinking of the welfare of others. Whosoever has lost himself has found the universe and the inhabitants thereof. Whosoever is occupied with himself is wandering in the desert of heedlessness and regret. The 'master-key' to self-mastery is self-forgetting. The road to the palace of life is through the path of renunciation." [17]

> "He has endowed us with a power to penetrate the realities of things; but we must be self-abnegating, we must have pure spirits, pure intentions, and strive with heart and soul while in the human world to attain everlasting glory." [18]

> "Wherefore must the veils of the satanic self be burned away at the fire of love, that the spirit may be purified and cleansed and thus may know the station of the Lord of the Worlds." [19]

> "Leave all thought of self, and strive only to be obedient and submissive to the Will of God. In this way only shall we become citizens of the Kingdom of God, and attain unto life everlasting." [20]

> "Do all ye can to become wholly weary of self, and bind yourselves to that Countenance of Splendors; and once ye have reached such heights of servitude, ye will find, gathered within your shadow, all created things. This is boundless grace; this is the highest sovereignty; this is the life that dieth not. All else save this is at the last but manifest perdition and great loss." [21]

> "Wherefore, O friend, give up thy self that thou mayest find the Peerless One, pass by this mortal earth that thou mayest seek a home in the nest of heaven. Be as naught, if thou wouldst kindle the fire of being and be fit for the pathway of love." [22]

> "Let us put aside all thoughts of self; let us close our eyes to all on earth, let us neither make known our sufferings nor complain of our wrongs. Rather let us become oblivious of our own selves, and drinking down the wine of heavenly grace, let us cry out our joy, and lose ourselves in the beauty of the All-Glorious." [23]

**"O people of the world! Follow not the promptings of the self, for it summoneth insistently to wickedness and lust; follow, rather, Him Who is the Possessor of all created things, Who biddeth you to show forth piety, and manifest the fear of God."** [24]

The attitudes suggested by the above passages stand in sharp contrast to the idolization of self and the obsession with self-gratification so characteristic of many societies today. Identify from these passages some of the attitudes we should develop towards self. Two examples are given to assist you.

—  We should learn <u>to renounce our own selves, forget our own opinions, cast aside personalities and be thinking of the welfare of others.</u>

—  We should learn <u>to be self-abnegating.</u>

—  We should learn _____

—  We should learn _____

—  We should learn _____

—  We should learn _____

—  We should learn _____

—  We should learn _____

Discuss in your group how the attitudes you have identified contribute towards the development of a noble being and endow acts of service with power.

# SECTION 8

Finally, the following words of 'Abdu'l-Bahá remind us of the reciprocal relationship between self-sacrifice and the ability to contribute to the transformation of society:

"The mass of the people are occupied with self and worldly desire, are immersed in the ocean of the nether world and are captives of the world of nature, save those souls who have been freed from the chains and fetters of the material world and, like unto swift-flying birds, are soaring in this unbounded realm. They are awake and vigilant, they shun the obscurity of the world of nature, their highest wish centereth on the eradication from among men of the struggle for existence, the shining forth of the spirituality and the love of the realm on high, the exercise of utmost kindness among peoples, the realization of an intimate and close connection between religions and the practice of the ideal of self-sacrifice. Then will the world of humanity be transformed into the Kingdom of God." [25]

"O army of God! Today, in this world, every people is wandering astray in its own desert, moving here and there according to the dictates of its fancies and whims, pursuing its own particular caprice. Amongst all the teeming masses of the earth, only this community of the Most Great Name is free and clear of human schemes and hath no selfish purpose to promote. Alone amongst them all, this people hath arisen with aims purified of self, following the Teachings of God, most eagerly toiling and striving toward a single goal: to turn this nether dust into high heaven, to make of this world a mirror for the Kingdom, to change this world into a different world, and cause all humankind to adopt the ways of righteousness and a new manner of life." [26]

"O ye loved ones of God! In this, the Bahá'í dispensation, God's Cause is spirit unalloyed. His Cause belongeth not to the material world. It cometh neither for strife nor war, nor for acts of mischief or of shame; it is neither for quarreling with other Faiths, nor for conflicts with the nations. Its only army is the love of God, its only joy the clear wine of His knowledge, its only battle the expounding of the Truth; its one crusade is against the insistent self, the evil promptings of the human heart. Its victory is to submit and yield, and to be selfless is its everlasting glory." [27]

The above passages describe some of the distinguishing qualities of those whom 'Abdu'l-Bahá considers to be in the "army of God", to whom He refers as the "loved ones of God", those who are "freed from the chains and fetters of the material world". Reflect on these distinctions as you complete the sentences below.

a.  The mass of the people are occupied with _____ ,

    are immersed in _____

    and are captives _____ .

b.  Those souls who have been freed from the chains and fetters of the material

    world and who, like unto swift-flying birds, are soaring in this unbounded

    realm are _____ and _____ ; they shun _____

    _____ , and their highest wish centers

    on the _____

    _____ , _____

_____ and _____ ,

the exercise of _____ ,

the realization of _____

_____ and the practice of _____

_____ .

c.  Today, in this world, every people is _____

_____ , moving _____

_____

_____ , pursuing _____ .

d.  Only this community of the Most Great Name is _____

_____ and has _____

_____ . Alone amongst them all, this people has arisen with _____

_____ , following _____ ,

most eagerly _____

_____ : to turn _____ into _____ ,

to make _____ a _____ ,

to change _____ into a _____ ,

and cause all humankind _____

_____ .

e.  God's Cause is spirit _____ . It belongs not to the _____

_____ . Its only army is _____ , its only

joy _____ , its only battle

_____ ; its one crusade is

_____ , _____

_____ . Its victory is to _____

_____ , and to be _____

_____ .

# SECTION 9

You may wish to memorize the following excerpts from prayers revealed by Bahá'u'lláh:

**"Inspire them, O my Lord, with a sense of their own powerlessness before Him Who is the Manifestation of Thy Self, and teach them to recognize the poverty of their own nature in the face of the manifold tokens of Thy self-sufficiency**

and riches, that they may gather together round Thy Cause, and cling to the hem of Thy mercy, and cleave to the cord of the good pleasure of Thy will." [28]

"Divest, then, Thy servants, O my God, of the garments of self and desire, or grant that the eyes of Thy people may be lifted up to such heights that they will discern in their desires naught except the stirring of the gentle winds of Thine eternal glory, and may recognize in their own selves nothing but the revelation of Thine own merciful Self, that the earth and all that is therein may be cleansed of whatever is alien to Thee, or anything that manifesteth aught save Thy Self." [29]

# SECTION 10

As your interest in nurturing junior youth deepens, you will become familiar with the many theories that attempt to describe adolescence. One of the words you will repeatedly encounter is "crisis"—related to identity, emotions, relations with parents, interactions with authority, and so on. You need to look critically at these theories, lest you come to regard a state of crisis as a necessary condition of every junior youth. Is it essential for the life of every adolescent to be characterized primarily by upheavals of one kind or another? Have junior youth throughout history experienced turmoil and confusion, and do they go through such crises in every culture and society today?

In trying to answer these questions, you should be aware that most prevalent studies of young people are carried out within frameworks that place excessive emphasis on self, on gratification, on biological change, on sexual awareness, and on material achievements— career, income, and social status. They often focus narrowly on class, race, and gender, neglecting the God-given qualities inherent in every human soul. Some of the insights you gain from these studies will, of course, be of assistance as you endeavor to understand the characteristics of this age group. But it is doubtful that efforts inspired by such studies can do much more than acculturate young people to the norms of a materialistic society, a society whose outlook, we know, tends to destroy spiritual susceptibilities. By contrast, would not the conception of junior youth you embrace call for the development of the spiritual identity of individuals who will "carry forward an ever-advancing civilization" and who will become "builders of unity" and "champions of justice".

What is important to remember in this respect is that the way young people are seen by others has an enormous effect on them. Thus the dark picture of adolescence becoming so widespread in society helps to foster the conditions for undesirable patterns of behavior to be propagated. Take, for example, the statement attributed to Sigmund Freud that adolescence is a temporary mental illness or Anna Freud's suggestion that being normal during the adolescent period is by itself abnormal. Do not such statements act as veils that prevent people from seeing the true capacity of junior youth? What evidence led these scientists to such sweeping conclusions? There are, of course, a number of educators who have spoken of adolescence in more favorable terms, but their ideas do not dominate the discourse on the subject. The images that persist in the minds of parents and teachers alike are of rebelliousness, irrationality, and frivolity. How can a society that has these ideas flowing through its veins, we may ask, help adolescents to become the kind of youth described in the first unit of this book?

# SECTION 11

In the context of the discussion above, we would like to suggest that you adopt the following position: whenever any group of junior youth develops undesirable behavior—beyond that which results naturally from the successive stages of crisis and victory characteristic of the process of normal growth—its causes should be sought in the social environment, perhaps in the glaring contradictions that young awakening minds discover in the lives of adults who were previously trusted without reservation or in the inability of adults to recognize the rationality of an individual trying to leave behind the habits of childhood.

This position, of course, does not argue the total absence of impetuosity or rebelliousness in adolescent behavior. What is being suggested is that the social environment, particularly the conduct of adults, is largely responsible for many of the undesirable traits that have come to be associated with this age. The following passage written by the Universal House of Justice, addressed specifically to parents, speaks to this point:

> **"What needs to be appreciated in this respect is the extent to which young minds are affected by the choices parents make for their own lives, when, no matter how unintentionally, no matter how innocently, such choices condone the passions of the world—its admiration for power, its adoration of status, its love of luxuries, its attachment to frivolous pursuits, its glorification of violence, and its obsession with self-gratification. It must be realized that the isolation and despair from which so many suffer are products of an environment ruled by an all-pervasive materialism."** [30]

To explore the implications of the claim we have made, you may wish to discuss in your group the validity of the following statements and compose others that further elaborate on the idea:

- Junior youth rebel against adults who ask them to follow standards which they themselves do not follow.

- Junior youth seem rebellious when given advice that is expressed in a moralizing tone.

- They become frivolous when the world offers them nothing but superficial activities that impede the development of their intellectual capacities.

- They show contempt for discipline when adults impose on them harsh rules, especially if they were given unrestricted freedom as children.

- They seem impulsive when adults around them do not know how to help them think through the consequences of their decisions.

- They develop pride when they are taught self-importance rather than selfless service to society.

- They become self-indulgent when constant propaganda is tempting them to satisfy their physical desires.

_____
_____
_____
_____
_____
_____
_____
_____
_____
_____
_____
_____
_____

# SECTION 12

The Universal House of Justice has spoken of the "laxity and depravity" of a "permissive society" and the need for youth to guard against its influence:

> ". . . the Cause of God will derive immense benefit when it is observed that the Bahá'ís, and particularly Bahá'í youth, stand out against the laxity and depravity of the permissive society, that the exalted standards of conduct which they strive to uphold are firmly rooted in spiritual principles, giving them confidence, self-respect and true happiness. On the other hand only the greatest harm can be done to the Cause if its followers are simply engulfed by the current tide." [31]

In the following passage, the Guardian offers us profound insight into the nature of such a society and the influence it exerts on all of us:

> "Indeed, the chief reason for the evils now rampant in society is a lack of spirituality. The materialistic civilization of our age has so much absorbed the energy and interest of mankind, that people in general no longer feel the necessity of raising themselves above the forces and conditions of their daily material existence. There is not sufficient demand for things that we should call spiritual to differentiate them from the needs and requirements of our physical existence." [32]

There are a number of signs of moral downfall that the Guardian identifies when he describes the destructive forces operating in society today. Among the conditions he highlights in his communications are the irresponsible attitude towards marriage and the consequent rising tide of divorce; the weakening of family solidarity and progressive slackening of parental control; the feverish pursuit after earthly vanities, riches and pleasures; the lapse into luxurious indulgence; the degeneracy of art and music; the deterioration in the standard of literature and of the press; and racial animosity and patriotic arrogance. While no one is immune to the influences of these ills, they affect adolescents in a particular way. Think, for example, of some of the consequences of divorce. Young children undoubtedly feel profound sadness when their parents divorce, and they long for the safety and security of a united home. But it is as adolescents that individuals become overwhelmed by such emotions as guilt, anger, shame, and humiliation when the marriage of their parents breaks down. While they hold their parents responsible, they cannot help blaming themselves for the family misfortune. Seeds of skepticism towards marriage and family life are planted in their minds, and their pessimism is confirmed by the prevalence of divorce they observe in the society around them.

1. You may find it helpful to reflect on the manner in which some of the social conditions identified above can shape adolescents' perception of reality, the way they think about themselves, their views of life, their feelings and emotions, their ability to distinguish between right and wrong, their behavior towards others, and their confidence in the institutions of society. The various conditions mentioned are set out below, and some space is provided for you to write down your ideas.

   a. Laxity and depravity of a permissive society: _____

   _____

   _____

   _____

   _____

   _____

   _____

   _____

   _____

   b. Weakening of family solidarity and progressive slackening of parental control:

   _____

   _____

   _____

   _____

   _____

   _____

   _____

   c. Feverish pursuit after earthly vanities, riches and pleasures, and the lapse into luxurious indulgence: _____

   _____

   _____

   _____

_____

_____

_____

_____

_____

    d.  Degeneracy of art and music, and the deterioration in the standard of literature and of the press: _____

_____

_____

_____

_____

_____

_____

_____

    e.  Racial animosity and patriotic arrogance: _____

_____

_____

_____

_____

_____

_____

_____

2.      What sentiments fill your heart and mind as you reflect on how deteriorating social conditions affect the lives of junior youth? In what way does this awareness strengthen your efforts to help them develop the capacities inherent in their true nature?

# SECTION 13

To draw attention to the signs of a disintegrating world is not to deny the significance of the constructive forces that also operate in society today. What needs to be done is to offer junior youth an environment in which their spiritual powers can be nurtured, ensuring, in this way, that they are influenced by appropriate social forces. Any attempt to isolate them entirely from harmful social conditions would, of course, be futile. Every effort has to be made, instead, to enable them to assess and analyze the way the world around them affects their thoughts and emotions. In this connection, particular attention should be given to the question of propaganda, for, in most societies, propaganda is increasingly shaping the values, attitudes, and views of junior youth. A brief look at some features of advertising should suffice to illustrate this point.

The materialistic forces that govern propaganda distort reality. The images presented in advertisements, for example, of a perfect yet unattainable physical appearance play on the emotions of adolescents at a time of rising self-awareness. Message after message portrays the main occupation of young women as that of attracting men. Moreover, the tendency to define manhood purely in terms of physical power is exaggerated, often to the point of condoning violent acts and risk-taking and encouraging sexual adventures and conquests. Whatever is identified as weakness is heartlessly rejected, and aggressive behavior systematically propagated. Interestingly, a particular brand of toughness is projected as appealing, with the aim of inducing girls to adopt it.

There can be little doubt that the primary purpose of most advertising directed towards young people is to create a global culture to which they would yearn to belong. In this culture they would learn to speak a common language, behave in the same way, and above all, consume an inexhaustible array of products. More crucial still, they would be initiated into an elaborate value system that would determine their patterns of consumption for the rest of their lives. It is noteworthy that the term "teenager" itself was invented some decades ago to take advantage of the promising market this segment of society represents.

To fully exploit awakening desires, the culture that is being propagated by advertising places sexuality at the center of the life of a young person. Products such as soft drinks with no connection to sexuality are used to conjure up in the minds of the young illusions of romantic relationships. Feelings of personal inadequacy and the anxiety of being rejected because of body odor, imperfect skin, or unfashionable clothing are fostered in order to introduce cosmetic products and new styles that promise sexual appeal and freedom from embarrassment. Even automobiles are described by terms such as "hot", "handsome", "a honey to handle"—all with sexual connotations. As moral standards have declined over the past few decades, the morally objectionable content of advertising has become more and more explicit. Gradually, it would seem, certain aspects of consumerism are becoming forms of sexual activity in themselves.

The role of brands in the expanding global "teen" market deserves special mention. Studies that explore how to take advantage of the potential of this market unabashedly suggest that the worship of brand icons is a powerful element of consumerism. Apparently, brands provide an anchor in the uncertain world of adolescence. What is more, they are often seen as passports to the global youth culture made so appealing by advertising. The culture these marketing techniques promote is oblivious, of course, to rising poverty among the nations; it projects images of an abundance enjoyed by a minority of the world's population to convince young people from every background that consumer products are sources of limitless joy.

In certain studies of the "teen" market, young people are put into categories according to attributes that make them predisposed towards the consumption of specific kinds of products—categories that allow advertising to target them with greater effectiveness. In one particular study, for example, they are divided into six groups: the "Resigned", who perceive their fate as being sealed and who try to get by with a minimum degree of effort;

the "Thrills-and-Chills", who are seekers of pleasure and who, with minds free from social and political concerns, are ready to join in the worship of brand icons; the "Bootstrappers", who, though essentially like the preceding group, also possess drive and the capacity for hard work and see goods and services as a means to advance and maintain a competitive edge; the "Quiet Achievers", who are conformists that avoid political and social rebellion and remain closely linked with their families and who are discriminating buyers concerned with the quality and benefits of a product; the "Upholders", who are also conformists but not academically oriented and who fill their minds with sports statistics and the names of athletic teams and players, leaving little room for political and economic issues; and finally the "World Savers", who desire to make a positive change in the world and whose importance lies in the opportunity they offer marketers to turn social causes into commodities to be sold.

All things, it would seem, are susceptible to branding and consumerism. Yet, however disconcerting, the brief analysis presented above is not intended as a condemnation of advertising per se. Its purpose is to enhance your ability to examine propaganda critically—commercial, political, ethnic, cultural—so that you can assist junior youth in identifying its effects on their thoughts and behavior. The following three exercises may help you reflect further on this complex matter:

1.    Advertising uses language and imagery to transform ordinary products into sources of excitement. Symbols are used to give objects and events far greater significance than they deserve. A drink, for example, cannot simply be described as what it is—something that quenches thirst—but is portrayed as a harbinger of joy and fulfillment. The symbols employed by the fashion industry glamorize clothing and cosmetics. Symbols of youthful exuberance sell candy bars. Symbols of adventure and sportsmanship help promote cigarettes and liquor. Can you think of a few specific advertisements and the phrases and images they employ to make something into what it cannot possibly be?

_____

_____

_____

_____

_____

2.    The illusion of happiness created through the purchase of any given product would necessarily have to be short-lived, or else we would remain content with what we own. Advertising, therefore, has to constantly recreate desire and ensure that we are never satisfied and content. How is this achieved?

_____

_____

_____

_____

_____

3.    We have mentioned that even social causes are sometimes turned into consumer commodities. Can you give a few examples?

_____

_____

_____

_____

_____

# SECTION 14

A word of caution is necessary here. No matter how harmful the effects of present-day society on the young may be, it would be a mistake to overemphasize them in your endeavors. It is all too easy to fall into the habit of treating junior youth as delicate beings who have to be constantly protected from the ills of their environment. Such an approach will never lead to their spiritual empowerment. What should be the focus of your efforts is the realization of their potential to act as determined agents of social transformation and to contribute to the betterment of society. Even in the present troubled world, there are numerous examples of junior youth in every culture who have transcended the deplorable conditions of the environments in which they live and who have consistently demonstrated such attributes as enthusiasm for service, eagerness to learn, an acute sense of justice, and a strong tendency towards altruism.

A number of educators have described some of the innate intellectual and spiritual powers that manifest themselves during the transitional stage of adolescence. There are a few, for example, that have underscored the interest junior youth exhibit in theoretical problems not related to everyday realities. One educator has emphasized the role they can play in social change, calling each generation of adolescents "a vital regenerator in the process of evolution," that can "offer its loyalties and energies both to the conservation of that which continues to feel true and to the revolutionary correction of that which has lost its regenerative significance." And yet another thinker has likened those in adolescence to "empty but organic receptacles, fully formed though still growing," capable of receiving with all their "being", and has drawn attention to their potential to effect transformation. Convinced that education should take advantage of various modes of perception, including the intensity youth can bring to any experience, he has noted that such intensity, "together with integrity of being," can make of human society "a living, thriving, truly loving, joyously full and exuberant organism, rather than a cold, mechanical, empty theoretical concept." "That is the magic of transformation," are his words, "and that is the potential of adolescence."

These few references, together with the analysis undertaken over the last several sections, indicate how careful you need to be in articulating a conception of adolescence. While you will undoubtedly examine critically diverse views on the subject in the years ahead, your own understanding of the significance of this crucial period in human life will be largely shaped by passages from the writings such as those quoted in this and the previous unit. And there can be no doubt that your convictions will be confirmed by your own experience working with junior youth.

# SECTION 15

The materials that the Ruhi Institute recommends for study by junior youth, much like the books of its main sequence, appear deceptively simple at first glance. The simplicity lies largely in the language employed and in the exercises provided. The concepts treated are both complex and profound. The current of thought that runs throughout the materials, anything but childish, will challenge the junior youth who study them to reflect on issues deeply. To help you appreciate their capacity to do so, we are presenting you in this and the next two sections with a few ideas as expressed by several junior youth themselves, all of whom have been affected, in one way or another, by violence. So many images are projected in the media of the violent behavior of such adolescents that it behooves us to listen to some of their untold stories of loss and hope.

The first account is in the words of a thirteen-year-old boy—call him Peter to hide his real identity—who had seen the effects of violence and war since he was eight years old. When he was thirteen, he began to promote peace in schools and youth organizations, accepting the consequences, which included harsh ridicule from some of his peers:

> *None of it bothered me. My family believed it was important to care about the community and to do whatever we could to help. Even though I was only thirteen, I could see that the biggest problems facing us were violence and the war. Peace was needed more than anything else. Of course, it is hard for a child to try to make peace, but trying is the only way anything ever happens. . . .*

> *So many lies have been told in my country for so many years that people do not know what or who to believe anymore. They cannot always trust the newspapers, the radio or television, the politicians, the armed groups—but when they hear children talking about the violence and the way it affects us and how we want peace, somehow they know they are hearing the truth. . . .*

> *Some people say they are fighting for the poor, but the poor have suffered more than anyone else in the war. I think that some people are also fighting for revenge, or for power, or because they feel that they have no other choice. Some young people join the armed groups because their families are poor and they see no other way out.*

Peter and his family, threatened during ongoing civil strife, had to move out of their home. His father went back and forth between his office and the new town where they lived, but the relative calm they enjoyed could not be maintained. His father's active support of the processes of peace finally resulted in his assassination:

> *I thought I understood about war because I lived in the thick of the conflict. There were battles in the streets during the night. I was often woken up by gunfire. When I went to school in the morning, I saw the evidence—the blood on the sidewalks, the bullet-riddled buildings. And I had seen the victims at the morgue, not far from my father's office.*

> *I had talked about this with confidence, as if I knew what the war meant—but when my father was murdered, I was shattered not just by grief, but because then I understood the war. I knew what it felt like to want to fight. I realized that no matter how much you want peace, you take a step towards violence when the*

*war hits you personally. This is the same trap that has caught so many people in my country. . . .*

*Nothing was the same afterwards. The house felt like a dead empty shell. The streets that were so familiar all looked strange. Nothing and nowhere felt safe. I thought all my work for peace was worth nothing because it had not saved my father. The horrific violence that had engulfed our town had finally struck the heart of my family—and I had been unable to stop it. I blamed myself. I asked myself, "What had I done that my father should die in such a violent way?"*

The family continued to receive threats, and Peter bought a gun in order to protect his loved ones. One evening, about ten days after his father was killed, the members of Peter's family were gathered in a room on the upper floor of their house. As Peter came down to the kitchen, he saw an intruder with a gun in the garden looking up to the second floor windows:

*I knew that I could get my gun and kill this man. . . . It would be taking revenge for my father's death. I would be protecting my family. And almost no one in my country would blame me for shooting him . . . Yet while all of this was true I did nothing. . . . My father had wanted me to work for peace. How could I become violent now? The only way I could show respect and love for my father, the only way I could help save my family, was by trying to make peace. Killing the man would bring no peace to me, or my family or my country. In fact, by killing him I would lose everything. I would be no better than he was.*

Peter quietly watched the intruder, who, after a while and for no apparent reason, turned away and left. Not long after that incident, Peter got rid of his gun and vowed never again to acquire one.

Before reading the next account, you may wish to identify some of the qualities that distinguish Peter and say a few words about his capacity to reflect on profound subjects.

_____

_____

_____

_____

_____

_____

_____

# SECTION 16

Mary—also an assumed name—was raised in an environment in which there was a constant threat of conflict; she discovered the price of disagreeing with a group of friends at an early age:

*When I was eleven I was given the silent treatment myself, because I refused to take sides in an argument. A group of my friends had accused a girl in our class of stealing and a huge conflict erupted. You had to be either for this girl, or against her, and all my friends were against her. Everyone assumed I would stand by them, but there was no evidence that the girl was a thief. I couldn't be sure. I didn't want to oppose my friends, though, so I just said nothing. Everyone got mad and, for a whole year, no one spoke to me.*

Mary befriended a young man, and even though other girls teased her about him, she developed warm feelings towards him. They used to take long walks together and talk about their future until one day she found him cleaning a gun she did not know he owned:

*When I walked in, he gave me a smile, as if he were doing nothing out of the ordinary. I have always hated violence, hated guns, and hated the war. He tried to make excuses, the way people like that do, but I told him right away it was over between us. "I don't want this kind of life for myself or for my children," I said. I was so young it seems like a joke now but I felt like my world was breaking in two.*

Mary's school grades began to fall after this incident, and her mother grew concerned. Then one of her teachers reached out to her:

*Mr. . . . asked if I would like to talk things over. We went to a small café and over some strong coffee I spilled the whole story of my friend, the gun, the silence of my friends, the teasing of the girls, my embarrassment, and broken heart. He didn't laugh at me, or make me feel young and ridiculous. He treated me like an adult.*

*"You must understand," he told me, "that you hold your own future in your own hands. Your future does not belong to anyone else, not to your parents, and especially not to this boy. It is yours and you can make of it anything you want."*

At the age of fourteen, Mary was already a student leader at her school, promoting peace among her peers and the younger students. Here are some of the thoughts that occupied her mind in those days:

*We knew that ending poverty could help end the war, but we could do nothing about that. We knew that reducing unemployment would help, but we could do nothing about that either. We could not stop the bullets and the machetes. We could not end the violence. But we believed we could begin to build peace among ourselves. . . .*

*I knew that working for peace could be dangerous, and I was sensitive to anything that was out of the ordinary. Sometimes just the fear that anything bad could happen, especially to my family, made me weep and feel like running away. Yet the other children depended on me, and in a way I felt my own unborn children were depending on me too. I could not turn away, no matter how afraid I was. I could only be careful and try to stay safe.*

What are some of Mary's outstanding qualities?

_____

_____

_____

_____

_____

_____

_____

## SECTION 17

Here are accounts given by three other young people, each of whom expresses the noblest thoughts and the most tender emotions. The first is in the words of a sixteen-year-old girl, who, at the age of twelve, experienced the loss of a close friend that was caught in a gang fight and stabbed to death. She never forgot her friend and decided to dedicate herself to the promotion of peace. Later, she started to help children affected by violence:

> *Children as young as eight or nine years old joined gangs because they thought it was cool or because they thought the gangs would give them protection on the street. In a lot of cases they were just trying to escape from violence at home, but they found something even worse on the street.*

> *I have to take the bus to . . . , but most of the bus drivers know about the work I am trying to do. They charge only what I can afford for the fare and often let me ride for free. The road to . . . winds upwards, past rough shacks perched dangerously close to steep cliffs. The hills are deeply scarred where rocks have been removed for use in construction projects. Such work is hard, backbreaking, and poorly paid but many children from displaced families work on these sites. Their families have fallen into such deep poverty that the children drop out of school and do whatever they can to earn money.*

> *From the road, I walk ankle deep in slippery mud, across a makeshift footbridge that spans a stinking, contaminated river. The school consists of half a dozen dilapidated rooms, clustered under a tin roof. The wooden desks are battered and broken. Rubbish litters the sides of the classrooms. There is no electricity. One of the classrooms has only a skylight and no other windows. The floor is made of dirt. The rain thunders so noisily on the roof that everyone has to shout to be heard, and water leaks through everywhere. One classroom wall is decorated with paintings done by the children, of pretty houses that contrast sharply with their surroundings. Perhaps these are images of the homes they once had or that they long for in the future. . . .*

> *Many of the parents have sadness in their faces. They talk aggressively to their children, calling them names. But during the workshops they sometimes begin to change. Some of them think they have to beat their children to make them behave, but then they realize that beating can also drive a child away and onto the streets.*

The next paragraph provides the thoughts of a young girl who fled from home at the age of eleven, became addicted to drugs, was saved by the persistent help of a friend, and finally joined a youth movement dedicated to peace:

*It was so hard to explain what our lives were really like. I was afraid to admit that no matter how much you try to make peace, you can still get dragged back into violence. . . . I have always longed to escape from this life. It is hard to admit but right now I am once again slipping away from the peace movement. I have been lying to myself and pretending to my friends that everything is fine. This is not true. Sometimes I get high. Every night there are fights at home. If they are not yelling at me, my mother and stepfather are yelling at each other. I cannot stand it, so I escape to the streets, and there is a lot out there that can do a young person harm. . . . I walk two paths at the same time and I still wish I could walk the peace path all the time. I think that my struggle and the way I survived should be worth something. . . . I believe that young people would do a lot more to help peace if more adults were willing to cooperate, to listen to what we have learned and work with us. If we had peace at home, that would be a great beginning.*

The last passage describes the experience of a boy of fifteen whose brother was kidnapped by a revolutionary group. After some time, the family received news from him while in captivity, and they were allowed to correspond with him:

*I have sent poems to him, to inspire him to stay confident and hopeful. I tell him that I listen to his advice and study hard. I was very glad when he recently wrote back and said, "I am happy you're doing so well in school. . . . That's where I went wrong. I regret not having made the most of my studies. . . . I really didn't like reading, for example . . . yet here I have read over thirty books of all different kinds and there are still more to read. I even get the dictionary and look up weird words that I don't know. . . . I would never have done this of my own accord before. . . ."*

*Even though he seems safe, I still worry. If I could talk to the people who are holding my brother, I would ask them to have compassion and to understand the suffering they have caused.*

*I think that forgiveness is fundamental if we are to achieve peace. The war cannot come to an end without forgiveness. It is especially important for people like us who have suffered to forgive.*

*I think that this is what I am working for—I work for forgiveness.*

Discuss in your group some of the attributes exemplified by the youth cited in this section, and write down a few of your thoughts.

_____

_____

_____

_____

_____

_____

# SECTION 18

Finally, no exploration of the nature of adolescence, however brief, can ignore the life of Rúḥu'lláh, the young hero of the Faith who, at the age of twelve, joyfully drank from the cup of martyrdom. At the young age of seven, Rúḥu'lláh was granted the privilege of accompanying his father, Hand of the Cause of God Varqá, and his older brother on pilgrimage to the Holy Land. Rúḥu'lláh thrived spiritually in those sacred surroundings and basked in the sunshine of Bahá'u'lláh's presence. One day, we are told, Bahá'u'lláh asked Rúḥu'lláh, "What did you do today?"

"I was having lessons from [a certain teacher]" was the reply.

"What subject were you learning?" Bahá'u'lláh inquired further.

"Concerning the return [of the prophets]", Rúḥu'lláh responded.

"Will you explain what this means?" asked Bahá'u'lláh.

"By return is meant the return of realities and qualities," he answered.

"These are exactly the words of your teacher," Bahá'u'lláh observed. "Tell me in your own words your own understanding of the subject."

To this, Rúḥu'lláh replied: "It is like cutting a flower from a plant this year. Next year's flower will look exactly like this one, but it is not the same."

Rúḥu'lláh's intelligent answer pleased Bahá'u'lláh, Who often referred to him as Jináb-i-Muballigh (His honor, the Bahá'í teacher).

There are a number of other accounts that bring to light Rúḥu'lláh's sublime qualities. It is certainly true that, to scale the heights of sacrifice that he attained at the tender age of twelve, he could not have been any ordinary young person. Consecration to the Cause and sacrifice in the path of the Beloved need not, of course, be associated with martyrdom. Yet with what longing and boundless joy does Rúḥu'lláh describe their reality in his celebrated poem quoted, in part, below.

> From the cup of divine bounty give me to drink
> And rid me of sin and weakness;
> For though my sins be great indeed,
> The mercy of my Lord is greater still.
>
> Welcome to thee, cupbearer of the divine banquet!
> Come thou, refresh my soul and make
> Me worthy of being sacrificed
> In the path of the Beloved.

The junior youth in the group you will soon organize will not live the life of Rúḥu'lláh. The passages quoted in the past few sections, however, give an indication of what nobility a human being can manifest from a very young age. We are reminded of the statement made much earlier in this unit that rising awareness during adolescence can be directed towards one of two ends—towards submission to the Will of God and self-sacrificing service to humanity or towards captivity in the prison of self and passion. In the discussion that ensued over the next several sections, we explored the nature of adolescence, the potential of junior youth, and the effects of the environment on their lives. It may be opportune for you to pause here and write a few paragraphs on what you now consider to be the innate potentialities of junior youth and what needs to be done, if their spiritual and intellectual powers are to be developed.

_____

_____

_____

_____

_____

_____

_____

_____

_____

_____

_____

_____

_____

_____

_____

_____

_____

_____

_____

_____

_____

_____

_____

_____

_____

_____

_____

_____

# SECTION 19

Having explored over the greater part of this unit the potentialities of young adolescents, we should now say a few words about your participation in the junior youth spiritual empowerment program. One of the strongest yearnings of those in this age range is to belong to a group of peers. Youth find it reassuring to turn for advice to friends who understand and sympathize with them. It is a natural response to a legitimate need, then, that the program has been organized around the concept of a "junior youth group", the members of which meet together regularly and are guided systematically to act and to learn. The atmosphere of the meetings, while joyous, friendly and intimate, should not be frivolous. It should contribute, rather, to the enhancement of those qualities and attitudes that a life of service to the Cause and humanity requires. In such a setting, the members of the group, free from the fear of censure or ridicule, can express their thoughts and look for answers to the searching questions that occupy their minds. They learn to listen, to speak, to reflect, to analyze, to make decisions, and to act on them.

In each group, there is the need for an older person who, as a true friend to the youth, can assist them in developing their capacities. Those who perform this function are known as "animators". The presence of the animator helps the members of the group to remain hopeful and convinced that they can not only protect themselves against the forces of moral decay operating in the society around them but also contribute to its betterment. Although serving in this capacity is not the exclusive prerogative of any particular age, youth seventeen and above tend to make excellent animators since they find it easy to treat junior youth as equals, not as children, encouraging them to ask questions, raise doubts, and engage in the investigation of reality. In the passage below, 'Abdu'l-Bahá expresses His hope that youthful souls may be thus nurtured:

> **"It is the hope of 'Abdu'l-Bahá that those youthful souls in the schoolroom of the deeper knowledge will be tended by one who traineth them to love. May they all, throughout the reaches of the spirit, learn well of the hidden mysteries; so well that in the Kingdom of the All-Glorious, each one of them, even as a nightingale endowed with speech, will cry out the secrets of the Heavenly Realm, and like unto a longing lover pour forth his sore need and utter want of the Beloved."** [33]

A junior youth group is not a children's class. It has some of the features of a study circle, but its primary function is to serve as an environment of mutual support for its members, one in which they can develop the spiritual perception and patterns of thought and behavior that will characterize them throughout their lives. Having participated in the various courses of the Ruhi Institute, you have first-hand experience as a member of a study circle and have probably taught some classes to children in carrying out the practice component of the third course. Look at the list of characteristics below. For each, discuss in your group what similarities and differences you would expect to find between a junior youth group and a children's class, on the one hand, and a study circle, on the other.

- The nature of the group
- The relationship among the participants
- The atmosphere of the gatherings
- The role of the teacher, the animator, or the one serving as a tutor of the group

# SECTION 20

As you dedicate yourself to this area of service, you will soon realize that the efficacy of your efforts depends, to a great extent, on the quality of the relationship you establish with the members of any junior youth group. You will, of course, be prepared to listen to them, to offer them advice and, when necessary, to console them. Your strong belief in their integrity, and the respect and genuine love you have for each and every one of them, will create a special connection between you and the group. You will need to demonstrate your commitment to their well-being and progress, without the least trace of paternalism, self-righteousness, or authoritarian control—attitudes that leave no room for the junior youth to flourish. And you will have to take every opportunity to reinforce the foundation of true faith in their hearts and minds and to instill in them hope in a bright future. 'Abdu'l-Bahá exhorts us:

> **"First of all, be ready to sacrifice your lives for one another, to prefer the general well-being to your personal well-being. Create relationships that nothing can shake; form an assembly that nothing can break up; have a mind that never ceases acquiring riches that nothing can destroy. If love did not exist, what of reality would remain? It is the fire of the love of God which renders man superior to the animal. Strengthen this superior force through which is attained all the progress in the world."** [34]

Discuss how the following attitudes would disempower members of a junior youth group and what thoughts, sentiments, and conduct would help an animator to resist such tendencies.

Paternalism: _____

_____

_____

_____

_____

_____

_____

Self-righteousness: _____

_____

_____

_____

_____

_____

_____

_____

Authoritarian control: _____

_____

_____

_____

_____

_____

_____

## SECTION 21

Your relationship with the members of any group of junior youth will also be greatly affected by the example you set. The influence of example in the life of a young person cannot be overestimated. Our own efforts, then, to purify our hearts take on added significance in this connection. "Gross materialism"; "the attachment to worldly things that enshrouds the souls of men; the fears and anxieties that distract their minds; the pleasures and dissipations that fill their time; the prejudices and animosities that darken their outlook; the apathy and lethargy that paralyzes their spiritual faculties" are "among the formidable obstacles that", the Guardian states, "stand in the path of every would-be warrior in the service of Bahá'u'lláh". He reminds us further that our ability to resist such forces will depend on the degree to which we ourselves are cleansed of "these impurities," liberated from "these petty preoccupations and gnawing anxieties," freed from "these prejudices and antagonisms," "emptied of self," and "filled by the healing and the sustaining power of God".

What are some of the implications of the Guardian's exhortations for your efforts to contribute to the spiritual empowerment of junior youth?

_____

_____

_____

_____

_____

_____

_____

## SECTION 22

As a true friend to the junior youth as well as their wise advisor, it will be essential for you to accompany them during times of joy and through periods of difficulty. They will ever be in need of encouragement, if they are to scale greater and greater heights of excellence. To the extent that you focus on their achievements, rather than on shortcomings and mistakes, will you be able to assist them. You will give encouragement, but not, of course, in a way that boosts the ego. You will focus on accomplishments, yet not be afraid to offer advice if you see them in situations that could compromise their moral integrity.

To think about the nature of your friendship with the group, read the following excerpt from a letter written on behalf of the Guardian. Though it describes the relationship of the institutions of the Faith to the individual believer, it is relevant to your efforts as an animator of a junior youth group:

> **"The believers are, for the most part, young in the Cause, and if they make mistakes it is not half as important as if their spirit is crushed by being told all the time—do this and don't do that!"** [35]

Discuss why a young person's spirit can be crushed by being repeatedly reminded of his or her mistakes and by being constantly told what to do and what not to do. Write down some of your thoughts here.

_____

_____

_____

_____

_____

_____

_____

Encouragement is not the same as indiscriminate praise; it must be sincere and free from hypocrisy, otherwise it will lead either to pride or to lack of trust. Below are some examples of how 'Abdu'l-Bahá encouraged the believers in their efforts to serve the Cause.

> **"Verily I render thanks unto God for having aided you to serve His Cause in His great vineyard."** [36]

> **"Verily, I praise my supreme Lord for choosing you to call in His Name among the people, for attracting you to the beauty of the All-Glorious, and for strengthening you to render His Cause victorious."** [37]

> **"Verily, God purged thee of sins when He immersed thee in the sea of His mercy and gave thee to drink of the cup of faith and the pure wine of recognition. Well done! Well done! For thou hast yearned to surrender thy will to the will of God and hast longed to increase thy love for God, to broaden thy knowledge of Him, and to remain steadfast in His path."** [38]

> **"O my spiritual loved ones! Praise be to God, ye have thrust the veils aside and recognized the compassionate Beloved, and have hastened away from this abode to the placeless realm. Ye have pitched your tents in the world of God, and to glorify Him, the Self-Subsistent, ye have raised sweet voices and sung songs that pierced the heart. Well done! A thousand times well done! For ye have beheld the Light made manifest, and in your reborn beings ye have raised the cry, 'Blessed be the Lord, the best of all creators!'"** [39]

> **"O ye sincere ones, ye longing ones, ye who are drawn as if magnetized, ye who have risen up to serve the Cause of God, to exalt His Word and scatter His sweet savors far and wide! I have read your excellent letter, beautiful as to**

**style, eloquent as to words, profound as to meaning, and I praised God and thanked Him for having come to your aid and enabled you to serve Him in His widespreading vineyard."** [40]

**"Thy letter was like a perfumed bouquet of flowers shedding abroad the fragrance of faith and certitude. Well done! Well done! Thou hast turned thy face toward the unseen Kingdom. Splendid! Splendid! Thou wast attracted to the Beauty of the Almighty! Marvelous! Marvelous! How fortunate thou wast to have attained unto this supreme bounty!"** [41]

Inspired by the manner in which 'Abdu'l-Bahá praised the friends, describe in a few sentences how you will go about encouraging the members of the group you will soon be assisting.

_____

_____

_____

_____

_____

_____

_____

_____

# SECTION 23

Finally, you need to remember that your efforts to establish deep bonds of loving friendship with the members of a junior youth group and to encourage them to strive for excellence will bear fruit to the extent that you create a joyful environment.

**"Joy gives us wings! In times of joy our strength is more vital, our intellect keener, and our understanding less clouded. We seem better able to cope with the world and to find our sphere of usefulness."** [42]

In order to create a joyful environment for the group, you need to feel joy. Think of the group of junior youth with whom you will soon be working. What thoughts about them come to your mind that bring you joy?

_____

_____

_____

_____

_____

_____

_____

_____

What are some practical measures you can take in order to infuse with joy the meetings of a junior youth group, without making them frivolous?

_____

_____

_____

_____

_____

_____

_____

Let us bring our study of this unit to a close by reading the passage below from a letter written on behalf of the Universal House of Justice:

> "The inner joy that every individual seeks, unlike a passing emotion, is not contingent on outside influences; it is a condition, born of certitude and conscious knowledge, fostered by a pure heart, which is able to distinguish between that which has permanence and that which is superficial." [43]

With these thoughts in mind, then, reflect on the following words of 'Abdu'l-Bahá:

> "The greatest gift of man is universal love—that magnet which renders existence eternal. It attracts realities and diffuses life with infinite joy. If this love penetrate the heart of man, all the forces of the universe will be realized in him, for it is a divine power which transports him to a divine station and he will make no progress until he is illumined thereby. Strive to increase the love-power of reality, to make your hearts greater centers of attraction and to create new ideals and relationships." [44]

# REFERENCES

1.  From the Riḍván 2010 message written by the Universal House of Justice to the Bahá'ís of the world, published in *The Five Year Plan, 2011–2016: Messages of the Universal House of Justice* (West Palm Beach: Palabra Publications, 2013), pp. 10–11.

2.  *The Promulgation of Universal Peace: Talks Delivered by 'Abdu'l-Bahá during His Visit to the United States and Canada in 1912* (Wilmette: Bahá'í Publishing, 2012), p. 617.

3.  *Selections from the Writings of 'Abdu'l-Bahá* (Wilmette: Bahá'í Publishing Trust, 1997, 2009 printing), no. 111, pp. 144–45.

4.  *Abdul Baha on Divine Philosophy* (Boston: The Tudor Press, 1918), pp. 131–32.

5.  *Gleanings from the Writings of Bahá'u'lláh* (Wilmette: Bahá'í Publishing, 2005), no. 153, p. 370.

6.  Ibid., no. 1, p. 3.

7.  *Tablets of Bahá'u'lláh Revealed after the Kitáb-i-Aqdas* (Wilmette: Bahá'í Publishing Trust, 1988, 2005 printing), pp. 34–35.

8.  Bahá'u'lláh, *The Hidden Words* (Wilmette: Bahá'í Publishing Trust, 2003), Arabic no. 13, pp. 6–7.

9.  *Selections from the Writings of 'Abdu'l-Bahá*, no. 34, p. 73.

10. Ibid., no. 35, p. 77.

11. *Tablets of Abdul-Baha Abbas* (New York: Bahá'í Publishing Committee, 1909, 1930 printing), vol. 1, p. 136. (authorized translation)

12. 'Abdu'l-Bahá, *The Secret of Divine Civilization* (Wilmette: Bahá'í Publishing, 2007), p. 136.

13. *Selections from the Writings of 'Abdu'l-Bahá*, no. 68, p. 110.

14. Ibid., no. 155, p. 191.

15. *The Promulgation of Universal Peace*, p. 205.

16. Ibid., p. 258.

17. 'Abdu'l-Bahá, in *Bahai Scriptures: Selections from the Utterances of Baha'u'llah and Abdul Baha* (New York: Bahá'í Publishing Committee, 1928), no. 992, p. 548.

18. *The Promulgation of Universal Peace*, p. 261.

19.    Bahá'u'lláh, *The Seven Valleys and The Four Valleys* (Wilmette: Bahá'í Publishing Trust, 1991, 2004 printing), p. 11.

20.    *Paris Talks: Addresses Given by 'Abdu'l-Bahá in 1911* (Wilmette: Bahá'í Publishing, 2011), p. 53.

21.    *Selections from the Writings of 'Abdu'l-Bahá,* no. 36, p. 82.

22.    *The Seven Valleys and The Four Valleys,* pp. 9–10.

23.    *Selections from the Writings of 'Abdu'l-Bahá,* no. 195, p. 247.

24.    Bahá'u'lláh, *The Kitáb-i-Aqdas: The Most Holy Book* (Wilmette: Bahá'í Publishing Trust, 1993, 2009 printing), pp. 42–43.

25.    *Selections from the Writings of 'Abdu'l-Bahá,* no. 223, pp. 294–95.

26.    Ibid., no. 35, p. 75.

27.    Ibid., no. 206, p. 268.

28.    *Prayers and Meditations by Bahá'u'lláh* (Wilmette: Bahá'í Publishing Trust, 2013), no. 36, p. 38.

29.    Ibid., no. 184, p. 271.

30.    From a message dated 28 December 2010 written by the Universal House of Justice to the Conference of the Continental Boards of Counsellors, published in *The Five Year Plan, 2011–2016,* p. 53.

31.    From a letter dated 23 November 1983 written on behalf of the Universal House of Justice to an individual believer, published in *Lights of Guidance: A Bahá'í Reference File,* compiled by Helen Bassett Hornby (New Delhi: Bahá'í Publishing Trust, 1996, 2001 printing), pp. 359–60.

32.    From a letter dated 8 December 1935 written on behalf of Shoghi Effendi to an individual believer, published in *The Importance of Prayer, Meditation, and the Devotional Attitude*, compiled by the Research Department of the Universal House of Justice (New Delhi: Bahá'í Publishing Trust, 1997), p. 32.

33.    *Selections from the Writings of 'Abdu'l-Bahá,* no. 107, p. 141.

34.    *Abdul Baha on Divine Philosophy,* p. 112.

35.    From a letter dated 30 June 1957 written on behalf of Shoghi Effendi to a National Spiritual Assembly, in "The National Spiritual Assembly", published in *The Compilation of Compilations* (Maryborough: Bahá'í Publications Australia, 1991), vol. 2, p. 128.

36.    *Tablets of Abdul-Baha Abbas,* vol. 1, p. 11. (authorized translation)

37.   Ibid., p. 18. (authorized translation)

38.   *Tablets of Abdul-Baha Abbas* (New York: Bahá'í Publishing Committee, 1915, 1940 printing), vol. 2, pp. 266–67. (authorized translation)

39.   *Selections from the Writings of 'Abdu'l-Bahá,* no. 236, p. 332.

40.   Ibid., no. 199, p. 252.

41.   *Tablets of Abdul-Baha Abbas* (New York: Bahá'í Publishing Committee, 1916, 1930 printing), vol. 3, p. 530. (authorized translation)

42.   *Paris Talks,* p. 135.

43.   From an unpublished letter dated 19 April 2013 written on behalf of the Universal House of Justice to a small group of individual believers.

44.   *Abdul Baha on Divine Philosophy,* pp. 111–12.

# Serving as an Animator

## Purpose

To reflect on concepts that shape
the junior youth spiritual empowerment program.

## Practice

To join a more experienced animator
in a few meetings of a junior youth group
or to help, with the aid of such a friend if necessary,
several junior youth to come together as a group
and engage in the program.

# SECTION 1

In the second unit of this book we discussed the significance of the social environment in the life of a young person during early adolescence. The junior youth spiritual empowerment program has, accordingly, been organized around the concept of a "junior youth group". A junior youth group, we have said, is not a children's class. It has some of the features of a study circle, but its primary function is to serve as an environment of mutual support for its members, one in which they can develop the spiritual perception and patterns of thought and behavior that will characterize them throughout their lives.

Normally, a junior youth group meets once a week, though sometimes more, over a three-year period and studies materials that have been specifically developed for ages between twelve and fifteen. Studying occupies only a portion of the time the youth spend together. During the rest of the time, they consult on and plan service projects, participate in sports, and engage in cultural activities, such as drama and crafts, suited to their immediate surroundings. In addition to regular meetings, the group attends special events and undertakes acts of service to the community. In this unit, we will examine the various aspects of the program with which you should become familiar.

# SECTION 2

Let us consider first the membership of the group. When the junior youth of a community show interest in the program, it is usually possible to form a group of ten to fifteen members. While the ages of the majority will range between twelve and thirteen, some of the youth may be just under twelve and others as old as fourteen. Experience suggests that the program proves most effective when the members, whatever their ages, remain together for the entire three-year period and complete it as a group. At that point, those who wish can move in unison to the next stage of the educational process, studying the main sequence of institute courses and following the paths of service it opens to them.

In certain places the youth who join a group will have participated in Bahá'í children's classes, but it should be remembered that, in many circumstances, the young people who encounter the program will have had no previous contact with the Faith. Besides age difference, then, there will often be some variation in terms of background and experience. No group is ever homogeneous, and animators consistently face the challenge of responding to the varied interests of the youth. A great deal of flexibility and creativity is required in this respect, and you will need to be prepared to address this challenge every time you come together with a group. How would you, for example, deal with the following situations?

- Some members of the junior youth group you are assisting experience difficulty in their reading comprehension.

- Younger members of the group feel belittled when you try to work with them separately.

- One or two older members do not find certain activities of the group challenging enough.

- Some members of the group decline to participate in a particular activity.

- A few members of the group show the capacity to go through the material at a pace quicker than the rest.

- Girls and boys in the group are reluctant to participate in certain activities together.

- Several members do not have sufficient means to contribute, say, towards a group outing.

- One or two of the members are irregular in their attendance.

- One member makes inappropriate jokes during the meetings.

- A few members of the group bring their younger siblings along to the meetings.

- One or two of the members do not participate in group discussions.

Discuss in your group these and similar situations. Of course, as you gain experience in this area of service, you will explore such challenges time and again in periodic meetings of reflection with your fellow animators and will acquire fresh insights.

_____
_____
_____
_____
_____
_____
_____
_____
_____
_____
_____
_____
_____
_____
_____
_____
_____
_____
_____
_____

# SECTION 3

The books the study of which lies at the heart of the program are loosely arranged by level of difficulty, both in terms of language and concepts explored. It is expected that, as additional books become available, a more consolidated order will eventually emerge on the basis of experience. The texts are divided into two categories. Those in the first address themes from a Bahá'í perspective, but not in the mode of religious instruction. In this sense they may be called "Bahá'í inspired". They constitute a major component of the program. The other category includes texts, fewer in number, that provide a distinctly Bahá'í component. We will examine that component in the next section and will concentrate here on the nature of the Bahá'í-inspired texts.

In general, educational materials of this kind are created with the conviction that, in the ocean of Bahá'u'lláh's Revelation, there are innumerable pearls of wisdom that should be offered to interested individuals, even when they do not yet recognize His Station. You are already familiar with this concept as, in the third unit of Book 2, "Introducing Bahá'í Beliefs", you studied passages based on the talks and Tablets of 'Abdu'l-Bahá in order to develop the ability to integrate spiritual knowledge and insight thus gained into your daily conversations.

As you know from your own experience, in discussing with others the themes explored in that unit, you may on some occasions mention the source of your inspiration in a natural way, though, at times, you may think it best not to do so—this, according to the demands of each circumstance. The same principle applies in the case of Bahá'í-inspired material. A letter written on behalf of the Universal House of Justice notes in this connection:

> **"One of the basic principles governing Bahá'í social and economic development is that the friends should give the Teachings of Bahá'u'lláh liberally and unconditionally to humanity so that people everywhere can apply them to pressing social issues and improve their individual and collective lives, both in material and spiritual dimensions. Access to the Word of God should not be conditioned upon acceptance of Bahá'u'lláh as a Manifestation of God for today. Moreover, it would not be inappropriate to refrain from explicitly mentioning the Source of inspiration underlying an educational program developed on the basis of His Teachings, when circumstances demand it. In this light, there are a range of options that the friends can consider when creating educational materials which draw on the teachings and principles of the Faith."** [1]

And another letter written on behalf of the House of Justice states:

> **"We have been asked to inform you that there is no requirement to cite the author when using a quotation from the Bahá'í writings in Bahá'í-inspired curricula material if there appears to be a wisdom in not doing so."** [2]

Thus, while all Bahá'í-inspired material is developed under the direct influence of Bahá'u'lláh's Revelation, the nature of each set of materials and its intended use dictate the extent to which the Faith is to be explicitly mentioned. In some, it is quite appropriate to incorporate passages from the Sacred Texts. In others, Bahá'í teachings may be explained without any quotations. In either case, references to the original sources may or may not be included. It is important to realize, however, that even in cases where no explicit mention of the Faith is made, the context of the teaching-learning experience makes it clear that the material is indeed inspired by Bahá'u'lláh's Revelation.

The Bahá'í-inspired materials we are considering here draw extensively on the power of the Word of God, both by quoting directly from the writings and by weaving the teachings of the Faith into the presentation of intellectual, moral, and spiritual themes. The texts themselves do not provide references, and it is generally left for the animator to decide, in light of the circumstances of the group and its inclinations and interests, whether to mention the sources of the quotations and, if appropriate, at which point to do so. Below is an extract from a lesson of *Breezes of Confirmation,* usually the first book studied by junior youth groups. Read it and discuss in what sense it can be regarded as Bahá'í inspired.

---

Godwin has a classmate and a close friend whose name is Chishimba. He often visits the Mulengas, and tonight he is staying for dinner. The conversation at the table jumps from one subject to another. Musonda wants to bring up the subject of confirmation, and she is impatient. Finally, there are a few moments of silence. "Rose and I have been talking about confirmation," says Musonda.

"There goes my little sister," says Godwin, clearing his throat. But to his surprise, Chishimba looks interested.

"What does the word mean to you?" he asks Musonda.

Musonda, also surprised, looks at Rose, hoping that she will answer.

"Confirmation . . . God confirms us and helps us in what we do," says Rose.

Chishimba does not say anything for a while. There is sadness in his eyes. "A few months ago," he slowly begins, "my father lost his job. He is honest and responsible, and everyone knows it. For eighteen years he worked as a guard in a company, and then, all of a sudden, they fired him. We all know the reason. If they had kept him two more years, he would have retired and the company would have had to pay him his pension. We don't have a lot of savings. Even though my older brother helps us, it looks like I cannot go back to school next year because I cannot pay for my room and board. I really love school. I wonder why God does not help me."

Everyone looks in the direction of Mr. Mulenga, expecting him to answer this question.

---

Mr. Mulenga smiles and says, "That God confirms us when we make an effort does not mean that life is easy. Your lives will be full of difficulties, and unfortunately, many of them will be caused by injustice. But you will have to work hard, and even though things may not go the way you wish for a while, you should be sure of God's confirmation. He will especially confirm you in your efforts to do away with injustice." He turns to Chishimba and says, "Your family is united and hardworking. My heart tells me that things will change for you. You will finish your studies. Take my word for it."

In Sections 20 and 21 we will look at *Breezes of Confirmation* in some detail, but for now you may wish to discuss the following questions in your group:

1. What is the main spiritual concept addressed in the above conversation?

2. Is the concept presented in a way that can be understood by junior youth?

3. In the second unit of this book we thought about the dangers of placing too much emphasis on "self". How does an educational process that stresses the importance of making an effort and attracting God's confirmation differ from one organized around the notions of self-realization, self-discovery, and self-esteem as described in that unit?

4. Do all junior youth, irrespective of their background, including those from Bahá'í families, benefit from the study of the kind of Bahá'í-inspired material being considered here? Why?


## SECTION 4

Texts in the second category provide content for the continuation of spiritual education received in Bahá'í children's classes. They are explicit in their treatment of fundamental Bahá'í beliefs and discuss the manner in which these beliefs are to be translated into action in the context of community life. The recognition of Bahá'u'lláh as the Manifestation of God for this age, identification with His purpose for humanity, obedience to His laws, firmness in the Covenant, and active participation in the life of the community are among the themes addressed.

In thinking about this category of materials, you will find the following passage written on behalf of the Guardian helpful:

"... the dangers facing the modern youth are becoming increasingly grave, and call for immediate solution. But, as experience clearly shows, the remedy to this truly sad and perplexing situation is not to be found in traditional and ecclesiastical religion. The dogmatism of the Church has been discarded once for all. What can control youth and save it from the pitfalls of the crass materialism of the age is the power of a genuine, constructive and living Faith such as the one revealed to the world by Bahá'u'lláh. Religion, as in the past, is still the world's sole hope, but not that form of religion which our ecclesiastical leaders strive vainly to preach. Divorced from true religion, morals lose their effectiveness and cease to guide and control man's individual and social life. But when true religion is combined with true ethics, then moral progress becomes a possibility and not a mere ideal." [3]

The above passage makes clear that, in contrast to the diminishing influence of traditional religion, the power of a living Faith can protect youth from "the pitfalls of the crass materialism" so rampant in society today. This power should be reflected both in the content of what young people study and in the way they are assisted in developing their spiritual capacities. To consider these ideas further, let us look at an extract from *Spirit of Faith*—one of the texts belonging to the category being examined here.

*Spirit of Faith* deals with themes philosophical in nature, for young people in this age range invariably grapple with fundamental questions of existence, questions which must be answered properly if confusion and even loss of faith are to be avoided later in life. It is in the Bahá'í teachings that answers are to be found to the many puzzling questions that baffle the human mind: the true nature of the human being, good and evil, free will and destiny, evolution and the appearance of the spirit of man, human intellect, and the spirit of faith. The book draws on insights gleaned from the writings, particularly from the penetrating explanations of 'Abdu'l-Bahá in *Some Answered Questions*, in order to shed light on these themes. It develops each theme through the conversations of a group of junior youth during their weekly meetings. The following section is taken from a lesson in which the youth are discussing the question of fate with the animator of their group, Natalia Petrovna:

"Let us see what we have understood up to now," says Natalia Petrovna. "We have the free will to do good or bad, and we have to use our volition to lead a noble life. But to have free will does not mean we can control everything. Things are bound to happen to us over which we have little control. Now I want to ask you about another idea. What do you understand by the word 'fate'?"

"I think fate is something we cannot change in our lives, no matter what," responds Igor.

"That sounds good. Can anyone give a few examples?" asks Natalia.

"We do not choose our parents," says Nadya.

"We cannot choose where we are born," adds Anton.

"My parents keep saying it is my fate to become a great pianist," says Vadik.

"But you don't have to. You can choose to become something else," says Marina.

"That is right. Fate is not that simple," says Natalia. "There is a good analogy that explains how fate works. Have any of you ever seen how a carpet is woven?"

There is a blank look on everyone's face, so Natalia continues: "Well, there is a frame. On this frame, or loom, parallel strands of yarn are stretched tightly from one end to the other. The weaver uses a variety of yarns of different colors to weave through these strands and create a pattern. One of the early believers once heard 'Abdu'l-Bahá say that we are all like weavers. We have been given the frame and the strands. We have also been given the yarns necessary for weaving, which you could say are all the talents and powers we are born with. This is our fate. But we choose the design that is to be woven on the loom. We have freedom over our actions. Each action creates a small part of the pattern. The complete work is who we grow up to be. Through free will and volition, we develop the powers and talents God has bestowed upon us."

---

**Reflections:**

God has given us all certain talents and capacities. One person may be good in biology, while another may have a talent for music. But we all have been given that which we need to develop as noble beings. It is not correct, then, to blame fate for our shortcomings. When we do that, we stop trying to improve ourselves. For each of the situations below, select the thought that will help the individual to change his or her circumstances.

a.  Someone often gets sick because he usually eats unhealthy food. He thinks:

    \_\_\_\_\_ It is my fate to be weak and sickly.

    \_\_\_\_\_ I should stop making excuses and change my eating habits.

b.  Someone does not study, so she performs poorly on her exams. She thinks:

    \_\_\_\_\_ I may not be the top student, but with diligence I will improve.

    \_\_\_\_\_ It is not my fate to succeed in school.

c. Someone gets drunk every time he faces a difficulty. When he is sober he thinks:

_____ Life forces me to drink.

_____ I can handle the problems in my life; I don't need alcohol.

d. Someone is in the habit of criticizing her friends, so they avoid her. She thinks:

_____ No one likes me.

_____ I should stop criticizing my friends and see the good in people.

e. Someone cheats on an exam and gets caught. He thinks:

_____ Isn't that just my luck! Others cheat and never get caught.

_____ How could I possibly do such a thing? I am supposed to adorn myself with the robe of honesty.

---

"Are we saying that it is no one's fate to become a criminal?" asks Ivan.

"Of course it is not," replies Natalia Petrovna. "In the analogy I just used, everyone can weave beautiful patterns with the frame and yarns he or she has been given. Though different, we all have the capacity to develop our characters and be good people."

Ivan agrees with all that is being said. Yet, something is bothering him and he does not exactly know what it is. Then suddenly he hears himself saying, "But this is all too hard."

No one quite understands what Ivan means.

"What is so hard?" asks Natalia.

"Making so much effort all the time to be strong, to be good," answers Ivan.

"You are right Ivan," says Natalia as she contemplates his answer. "But remember that God is aiding us all the time. He never leaves us alone. Think of a sailboat; the power to move it comes from the wind, not from the boat itself. But it is the captain who must catch the wind in the sail and steer the boat to its destination. All power comes from God. Without His aid, we are powerless. When we only look at ourselves, all we see is weakness. But when we turn to God and implore His aid and assistance, we find the strength to do what is pleasing to Him."

The youth then form pairs in order to memorize the following passages:

> **"The incomparable Creator hath created all men from one same substance, and hath exalted their reality above the rest of His creatures. Success or failure, gain or loss, must, therefore, depend upon man's own exertions. The more he striveth, the greater will be his progress."**

> **"O my God! O my God! Thou seest me in my lowliness and weakness, occupied with the greatest undertaking, determined to raise Thy word among the masses and to spread Thy teachings among Thy peoples. How can I succeed unless Thou assist me with the breath of the Holy Spirit, help me to triumph by the hosts of Thy glorious kingdom, and shower upon me Thy confirmations, which alone can change a gnat into an eagle, a drop of water into rivers and seas, and an atom into lights and suns? O my Lord! Assist me with Thy triumphant and effective might, so that my tongue may utter Thy praises and attributes among all people and my soul overflow with the wine of Thy love and knowledge.**

> **"Thou art the Omnipotent and the Doer of whatsoever Thou willest."**

Though you will have an opportunity to study the entire text of *Spirit of Faith* in Section 22, it would be fruitful to pause here and examine the content of the above extract by discussing the following points:

1.  How does the material present the concept of fate? Is it dogmatic?

2.  What would a dogmatic presentation of the concept be like?

3.  Does the material place the proper emphasis on helping junior youth to explore spiritual concepts, or are ideas presented rigidly?

4.  How does the material assist them in seeing the implications of the writings related to fate and free will for their lives?

5.  Does the story demonstrate tolerance for the differing views and emotions of the junior youth who are trying to understand the concepts? If so, how is it shown?

6.  What would happen if junior youth were not allowed to express their ideas freely in this respect?

7. How does Natalia Petrovna assist the junior youth in developing clarity of thought?

8. Are the questions discussed between the members of the group relevant to all junior youth, irrespective of their background?

# SECTION 5

Early adolescence is a period of life during which our capacity to look beyond the outer appearance of things is greatly enhanced; we seek a deeper understanding of what we witness and what we experience. This implies that junior youth are in need of spiritual perception; they should be assisted in recognizing spiritual forces, in seeing the spiritual reality of every condition, and in identifying relevant spiritual principles. In the writings, there are many references to seeing with the "eye of the soul", to opening the "inner vision", and to developing "inward sight". Thus, for example, does 'Abdu'l-Bahá counsel the Tarbíyat School in Ṭihrán:

> **"Let them make the greatest progress in the shortest span of time, let them open wide their eyes and uncover the inner realities of all things, become proficient in every art and skill, and learn to comprehend the secrets of all things even as they are—this faculty being one of the clearly evident effects of servitude to the Holy Threshold."** [4]

'Abdu'l-Bahá names spiritual perception as one of the powers that distinguish human beings from animals:

> **"It is clearly evident that while man possesses powers in common with the animal, he is distinguished from the animal by intellectual attainment, spiritual perception, the acquisition of virtues, capacity to receive the bestowals of Divinity, lordly bounty and emanations of heavenly mercy. This is the adornment of man, his honor and sublimity. Humanity must strive toward this supreme station."** [5]

And He refers to our inner vision and inner hearing as spiritual graces:

> **"He has given us material gifts and spiritual graces, outer sight to view the lights of the sun and inner vision by which we may perceive the glory of God. He has designed the outer ear to enjoy the melodies of sound and the inner hearing wherewith we may hear the voice of our Creator."** [6]

On another occasion He reminds us how essential it is to open our inward sight:

> **"Our spiritual perception, our inward sight must be opened, so that we can see the signs and traces of God's spirit in everything. Everything can reflect to us the light of the Spirit."** [7]

And in this passage 'Abdu'l-Bahá describes for us one instance in which spiritual perception enhances understanding:

"The conception of annihilation is a factor in human degradation, a cause of human debasement and lowliness, a source of human fear and abjection. It has been conducive to the dispersion and weakening of human thought, whereas the realization of existence and continuity has upraised man to sublimity of ideals, established the foundations of human progress and stimulated the development of heavenly virtues; therefore, it behooves man to abandon thoughts of nonexistence and death, which are absolutely imaginary, and see himself ever-living, everlasting in the divine purpose of his creation. He must turn away from ideas which degrade the human soul so that day by day and hour by hour he may advance upward and higher to spiritual perception of the continuity of the human reality." [8]

Can you say a few words about how spiritual perception brings new dimensions to human understanding that are not accessible through the exercise of mental powers alone?

_____

_____

_____

_____

_____

_____

_____

_____

# SECTION 6

Having explored the necessity of possessing spiritual perception, we must now ask ourselves how it is developed. The question, of course, does not admit a simple answer, and we can only consider here a few relevant ideas.

It is clear that spiritual perception is an attribute of a pure heart. 'Abdu'l-Bahá tells us:

"The more pure and sanctified the heart of man becomes, the nearer it draws to God, and the light of the Sun of Reality is revealed within it. This light sets hearts aglow with the fire of the love of God, opens in them the doors of knowledge and unseals the divine mysteries so that spiritual discoveries are made possible." [9]

That the knowledge of God is vital for the development of spiritual perception is also evident:

"For in the existing knowledge of the reality of things there is material advantage, and through it outward civilization progresses; but the knowledge of God is the cause of spiritual progress and attraction, and through it the perception of truth, the exaltation of humanity, divine civilization, rightness of morals and illumination are obtained." [10]

And the love of God is clearly indispensable if inner sight is to be strengthened:

> "O my friend! Render thou thanks unto God for having illumined thy sight with the effulgent rays shed from the Sun of Truth, and for having quickened thee and baptized thee with the water of life and the fire of the love of God." [11]

> "The love of God is spoken of as fire, for it burneth away the veils, and as water, for it is the source of life. In short, the love of God is the inmost reality of the virtues of the world of humanity. Through it, human nature is purified. Through the love of God, one is delivered from the defects of the human world. Through the love of God, one maketh progress in the realm of virtues. The love of God is the cause of the illumination of the world." [12]

You may find these exercises helpful as you reflect on the significance of the above counsels.

1.    Write a few sentences describing how each of the following enhances spiritual perception:

      a.  Purity of heart: _____

      _____

      _____

      _____

      b.  Knowledge of God: _____

      _____

      _____

      _____

      c.  Love of God: _____

      _____

      _____

      _____

2.    Decide whether the following statements are true or false:

      a.  Through reasoning alone, without the aid of the teachings of God, we are able to distinguish right from wrong.    T ☐  F ☐

      b.  It is the recognition of the Manifestations of God and obedience to their teachings that enable us to perceive truth.    T ☐  F ☐

      c.  Purity of heart makes a human being naive.    T ☐  F ☐

      d.  The more pure the heart, the more faithfully it reflects divine attributes, the light of which enables it to perceive the inner reality of things.    T ☐  F ☐

e.  The fire of the love of God burns away the veil of self, thus enabling the inner sight to behold the truth.　　　T ☐　F ☐

f.  The power of the love of God assists us in striving with a clear vision to abide by His Will and to fulfill His purpose.　　　T ☐　F ☐

g.  Fear of extinction weakens our intellectual and spiritual abilities, and therefore our spiritual perception is sharpened when we are convinced of the continuity of our existence.　　　T ☐　F ☐

h.  Selfless service to the Divine Threshold will assist us in seeing the inner reality of things.　　　T ☐　F ☐

i.  With inner sight, we can see divine confirmations.　　　T ☐　F ☐

# SECTION 7

The last quotation in the preceding section points to a fundamental concept of particular relevance to our exploration—namely, that numerous veils hinder the inner eye from seeing the reality of things. The development of spiritual perception entails the removal of such veils. 'Abdu'l-Bahá indicates:

> "The bestowals of God which are manifest in all phenomenal life are sometimes hidden by intervening veils of mental and mortal vision which render man spiritually blind and incapable, but when those scales are removed and the veils rent asunder, then the great signs of God will become visible, and he will witness the eternal light filling the world. The bestowals of God are all and always manifest. The promises of heaven are ever present. The favors of God are all-surrounding, but should the conscious eye of the soul of man remain veiled and darkened, he will be led to deny these universal signs and remain deprived of these manifestations of divine bounty. Therefore, we must endeavor with heart and soul in order that the veil covering the eye of inner vision may be removed, that we may behold the manifestations of the signs of God, discern His mysterious graces and realize that material blessings as compared with spiritual bounties are as nothing." [13]

Literal interpretation, vain imaginings, imitation, the self, and the pursuit of passion and desire are among the veils mentioned by 'Abdu'l-Bahá. So, too, can our material senses act as veils.

> "My prayer for you is that your spiritual faculties and aspirations may daily increase, and that you will never allow the material senses to veil from your eyes the glories of the Heavenly Illumination." [14]

> "One of the veils is literal interpretation. To penetrate the inner significances a mighty effort is needed." [15]

"Praise thou God that thou hast found thy way into the Kingdom of Splendors, and hast rent asunder the veil of vain imaginings, and that the core of the inner mystery hath been made known unto thee." [16]

"I fervently supplicate God to remove the veil from thine inner eye; to reveal to thee His most mighty signs; and to make thee a banner of guidance, wholly detached from all else but Him, ablaze with the fire of His love, occupied with His remembrance, and conscious of the realities of all things, that thou mayest see with thine own eyes, hear with thine own ears, and refrain from imitating any of thy forefathers. Look thou with insight into the Cause of thy Lord, for the people are wrapped in veils of darkness." [17]

". . . for there is no veil more obstructive than the self, and however tenuous that veil may be, at the last it will completely shut a person out, and deprive him of his portion of eternal grace." [18]

"Yet the pursuit of passion and desire will wrap the eyes in a thousand veils that rise out of the heart to blind the sight and the insight as well." [19]

In the first passage above, 'Abdu'l-Bahá tells us that "the bestowals of God are all and always manifest", "the promises of heaven are ever present", and "the favors of God are all-surrounding". He explains further that, "should the conscious eye of the soul of man remain veiled and darkened", he will be led to deny the great signs of God and will be deprived of these manifest bounties.

1.  What do you think are some of the bestowals and favors to which 'Abdu'l-Bahá is referring? _____

    _____

    _____

    _____

2.  Now describe how the veils mentioned below deprive us from beholding these bestowals and favors.

    a.  Literal interpretation of the sacred texts: _____

        _____

        _____

        _____

    b.  Vain imaginings: _____

        _____

        _____

        _____

    c.  Imitation: _____

        _____

d. Self: _____

_____

_____

_____

e. Pursuit of passion and desire: _____

_____

_____

_____

3. Decide whether the following statements are true or false:

a. Our inner eye perceives even without the aid of our mental
faculties and physical eyes.                    T ☐ F ☐

b. Our physical senses and mental faculties always hinder us
from perceiving spiritual reality.              T ☐ F ☐

c. Purifying our physical senses of all that does not pertain to
God assists our inner faculties in perceiving the truth.   T ☐ F ☐

4. Finally, reflect on this statement from the Writings of 'Abdu'l-Bahá to gain further
insight into the nature of the veils that can inhibit spiritual perception. Memorize
it if you wish.

**"Know thou, verily, there are many veils in which the Truth is enveloped:
gloomy veils; then delicate and transparent veils; then the envelopment of
Light, the sight of which dazzles the eyes, as doth the sun which is enveloped
only in its own light and, as we look at it, the sight is blinded and eyes are
dazzled.**

**"I beg of God to remove all the veilings and familiarize the light with all eyes,
so that man may not be veiled from witnessing the Sun of Truth." [20]**

# SECTION 8

Below is one of the lessons from *Glimmerings of Hope,* another Bahá'í-inspired
text studied by junior youth. It tells the story of Kibomi, a twelve-year-old boy who, after
the loss of his parents, embarks on a journey in search of his sister. Kibomi belongs to
the Adumbu tribe. His parents were killed in the midst of civil strife by members of the
Kungu tribe. The lesson immediately preceding this one describes his encounter with an
old man from the Kungu tribe who treats him with great kindness. Here he meets a group
of soldiers from his own tribe.

With some food in him, Kibomi has more energy and moves faster. When he ran from his village, he felt mostly fear and anger. Now he is beginning to recover the good feelings he has always had about people. The old man was a Kungu, but he was kind and wise. He shared his food. The words he spoke were beautiful and full of hope: "We have to make choices." "We were created to love, not to hate."

Kibomi continues to follow the river towards Nangata. After walking for a while, he hears voices and quickly hides behind a large tree. A group of young men are approaching. They are speaking the Adumbu language. Kibomi is happy to hear his language and slowly steps out from behind the tree. The men are wearing uniforms. They are soldiers of the Adumbu rebel army. Some of them are quite young, and one looks the same age as Kibomi. The soldiers stop as soon as they see him and hold up their guns. "Wait!" says Kibomi. "I am Adumbu like you!"

"What are you doing out here alone?" asks their leader impatiently.

"The Kungu attacked our village and killed my parents. I had to run away," answers Kibomi.

"Come and join us then," says the leader. "We must teach the Kungu a lesson. Make them pay for what they did to your family."

Kibomi is tempted. He thinks a little and is about to accept. The boy soldier comes forward and extends to him his hand. Kibomi looks into his eyes and is disturbed by the despair he sees in them. He hesitates. "I may join you later," he says with his voice shaking. "But now I must go and find my sister."

As the soldiers walk away, one turns and says, "Remember! Fighting back is the only way." Kibomi does not answer.

## Questions

1. What did Kibomi feel when he left his village?
2. Why has his feeling changed after seeing the old man?
3. Why does Kibomi hide behind the tree?
4. Who are the young men in uniforms that he meets?
5. What does the leader ask Kibomi to do?
6. What does Kibomi see in the eyes of the boy soldier?

**Activities**

1.  Kibomi sees despair in the eyes of the young boy soldier who, fearful and angry like himself, has made a choice to fight and kill. We all have moments of sadness and despair. In such times, we should not choose dark paths but should look for the light that restores hope. Read the following prayer and meditate on its words:

    **"He is the Compassionate, the All-Bountiful! O God, my God! Thou seest me, Thou knowest me; Thou art my Haven and my Refuge. None have I sought nor any will I seek save Thee; no path have I trodden nor any will I tread but the path of Thy love. In the darksome night of despair, my eye turneth expectant and full of hope to the morn of Thy boundless favor and at the hour of dawn my drooping soul is refreshed and strengthened in remembrance of Thy beauty and perfection."**

    You may now wish to memorize the above prayer.

2.  For each of the following situations, decide which thoughts and actions will bring despair and which will restore hope:

    a.  You do poorly on one of the subjects in an exam. *Hope Despair*

        – You give up studying and spend most of your time playing. ☐ ☐

        – You tell yourself that you are stupid. ☐ ☐

        – You ask another student to help you. ☐ ☐

        – You are patient with yourself and try harder to understand the subject. ☐ ☐

        – You blame your teacher for not helping you more. ☐ ☐

    b.  You feel lonely and it seems that you do not have any friends. *Hope Despair*

        – You keep to yourself and feel sad most of the time. ☐ ☐

|  |  | Hope | Despair |
|---|---|---|---|
| – | You spend less time thinking about yourself and care more for others. | ☐ | ☐ |
| – | You think about the faults of others all the time. | ☐ | ☐ |
| – | You look for the good in other people. | ☐ | ☐ |
| – | You take the first step to speak and be friendly to others. | ☐ | ☐ |

c. You see jealousy and fighting among some of your relatives.

|  |  | Hope | Despair |
|---|---|---|---|
| – | You, too, feel jealous and fight with them. | ☐ | ☐ |
| – | You try to be more generous towards them. | ☐ | ☐ |
| – | You pray for the members of your family to become united. | ☐ | ☐ |
| – | You teach the children in your family about love and generosity. | ☐ | ☐ |
| – | You tell yourself there is nothing you can do to change your relatives. | ☐ | ☐ |

d. A friend does something to hurt you.

|  |  | Hope | Despair |
|---|---|---|---|
| – | You decide to take revenge and hurt your friend. | ☐ | ☐ |
| – | You forgive your friend. | ☐ | ☐ |
| – | You decide never to hurt someone like that. | ☐ | ☐ |
| – | You tell others what a bad person your friend is. | ☐ | ☐ |
| – | You end your friendship. | ☐ | ☐ |

Mention some of the spiritual truths that junior youth might discover in this lesson. How are the themes of hope and despair, which are likened to light and darkness, treated? In what ways do you think the story and the accompanying activities help to sharpen the spiritual perception of junior youth?

_____

_____

_____

_____

_____

_____

_____

_____

_____

_____

_____

_____

_____

_____

_____

## SECTION 9

"Hope" and "confirmation" are two examples of the many themes that a program for the spiritual empowerment of junior youth needs to address. Careful discussion of such themes can strengthen spiritual perception and contribute to the expansion of consciousness. 'Abdu'l-Bahá states:

> **"There are certain pillars which have been established as the unshakable supports of the Faith of God. The mightiest of these is learning and the use of the mind, the expansion of consciousness, and insight into the realities of the universe and the hidden mysteries of Almighty God."** [21]

A human being can live at different levels of consciousness. To be aware of the divine will and purpose, to recognize the forces that influence us and our communities, and to strive to dedicate our mental and spiritual powers to building a new world—these imply a higher state of consciousness than a life focused on material concerns. One of the main challenges of an animator of a junior youth group is to help its members reach higher and higher levels of consciousness. If they are to do so, youth need to understand those concepts that are associated with themes central to a spiritual life. So, too, must they increase their capacity to reflect on and analyze such concepts and apply them to their reality. In addition to hope and confirmation, what are some of the themes and related concepts that junior youth should make the object of their reflection?

_____

_____

_____

_____

_____

_____

_____

_____

# SECTION 10

In the past few sections we have examined the question of spiritual perception and some of the attributes associated with it—purity of heart, the knowledge of God, and the love of God. We have also thought about the "veils" that can prevent us from seeing with our "inner eyes" and have considered how an understanding of certain concepts can help to strengthen our spiritual perception and expand our consciousness.

During adolescence the powers inherent in the human soul increasingly manifest themselves. Among these, the powers of thought and expression are of particular importance, and nurturing them is equally vital to the expansion of consciousness. There is an intimate connection between language and thought. The power of thought is revealed through utterance, and the enhancement of the power of utterance is indispensable to the cultivation of understanding. Developing the powers of expression and deepening one's understanding of reality go hand in hand. Understanding requires, after all, contemplation and reflection, activities inextricably bound up with language. Bahá'u'lláh states:

> **"O people of Bahá! The source of crafts, sciences and arts is the power of reflection. Make ye every effort that out of this ideal mine there may gleam forth such pearls of wisdom and utterance as will promote the well-being and harmony of all the kindreds of the earth."** [22]

Both understanding and the powers of expression are, of course, in need of illumination from Divine utterance. Bahá'u'lláh tells us:

> **"He hath come for your salvation, and hath borne tribulations that ye may ascend, by the ladder of utterance, unto the summit of understanding."** [23]

Enhancing the powers of expression involves more than the mere acquisition of the mechanical skills of reading, writing, and speech. It requires several abilities: to read with good comprehension, to describe ideas with clarity and eloquence, and to articulate concepts with reasonable precision. In the exercise of these abilities, junior youth learn to apply relevant scientific, moral, and spiritual concepts to the analysis of the world around them and to the formulation of personal convictions upon which their future social ideology can be built.

'Abdu'l-Bahá explains that "the mass of the population is uninformed as to these vital agencies which would constitute an immediate remedy for society's chronic ills". "At present," He also indicates, "because of their inadequate schooling, most of the population lack even the vocabulary to explain what they want." How fortunate, then, are those who, in early youth, are able to develop the powers of expression and, aware of the divine remedy for the chronic ills of humankind, fill their minds with heavenly thoughts, increasing in this way their understanding and expanding their consciousness.

In the lesson below from *Drawing on the Power of the Word,* a Bahá'í-inspired text often studied by junior youth that have already advanced through a number of earlier books, a group of young people are discussing the concept of the "word". Study the lesson and try to see how it increases understanding and raises consciousness.

One of the most exciting activities carried out by the Alegrías youth group in the first months of its existence was a tree-planting project. Once the youth had planted fifty fruit trees on the land surrounding their school, they invited their parents, friends and neighbors to a ceremony during which Elisa gave a short talk on the importance of improving the environment. The community appreciated this project because the trees they planted would bear fruit and beautify the village.

The day after the ceremony, before leaving Alegrías, Elisa asked for a special meeting with the youth. "Today I would like us to talk about a theme which will be at the center of our discussions for months to come," she told them with great enthusiasm. "To introduce it, let me ask you a question: Why do you think God created us?"

Mariela answered immediately, "God created us because He loves us. 'I loved thy creation, hence I created thee.' I learned this quote when I was a child and have never forgotten it."

"Excellent," responded Elisa. "God has created us out of His infinite love for us. And because of this love, He has bestowed upon each of us the most wonderful gifts. One of His greatest gifts to us is the ability to use the 'word'. No other living creature has been given the ability to speak words, read words, write words, and understand them. Through words, we communicate with each other and let each other know what we think and feel. Above all, it is in words that the divine teachings are expressed. We understand these teachings by listening to and reading the Word of God revealed through His Manifestation. The theme that I have in mind for our discussions, then, is the power of the word."

"I have heard that the word is more powerful than the sword," said Carlota.

"That's true," added Antonio. "But for words to have power, they must be accompanied by deeds. If not, words are empty and are easily swept away by the wind. One of my favorite quotes says that we should beware, lest we walk in the ways of them whose words differ from their deeds."

"Yes," added Ana Maria. "You can tell someone she's your best friend, but if you don't help her when she needs you, then perhaps you are not such a good friend after all."

Ana Maria's comment sparked everyone's imagination, and they all began to give examples of both empty words and words that are accompanied by deeds.

Finally Elisa said, "Good. You are all convinced that words accompanied by deeds are extremely powerful. Words have an incredible power—they can change the world. That is why you, who want to build a better world, should learn to use words well. This means thinking the word, understanding the word, speaking the word, spreading the word, and putting the word into practice."

For a while the youth remained quiet, reflecting on what Elisa had said. Then Diego suddenly had an idea. Excited, he jumped up in front of the group and said, "Now I know how we will achieve material and spiritual progress: by the power of the word accompanied by pure deeds."

Silence. No one said anything. Diego ended up just standing there, feeling uncomfortable. He did not know whether to sit down or remain standing. He looked to Elisa for help. Elisa got up slowly, went towards him, and took his hand. "You have discovered a very profound truth," she said to him. "Over time you will learn how important it is."

**EXERCISES**

1. Use the following words to complete the sentences below:

   > accompany, imagination, express, deeds, communicate, improve, bestowed, create, environment, surrounding, gift, revealed, convince, profound

   a. It is through the power of the word that we are able to _____ ourselves.

   b. Julia did not want her younger brother to go to the store alone, so she decided to _____ him.

   c. The doctor was happy to see that the young girl's health was beginning to _____ .

   d. Only by asking her several times did Luis Enrique finally _____ her to speak at the meeting.

e. God has given us the _____ of life, and we should not waste it.

f. Whenever Juan Carlos makes a promise, he tries his best to keep it. His words are always followed by _____ .

g. Because of His love for us, God has given us many gifts. The ability to use the word is one of the greatest gifts He has _____ upon us.

h. The short story was written entirely from the author's _____ .

i. In order to _____ with others, we should learn to listen.

j. Cecilia is concerned about the _____ and decided to give a course at her community center on sanitation.

k. Whenever there is a project to be done, Diego is able to get everyone excited about it. He is able to _____ enthusiasm.

l. Roberto was so tired after working hard all day that he went to bed and no one could wake him. He was in a _____ sleep.

m. My grandmother never liked to tell anyone how old she was, but when she turned 100 she finally _____ her age.

n. Anna planted a garden all round her house, so there were beautiful flowers of many different colors and shapes _____ it.

2. Write a sentence using each of the phrases below.

pure deeds: _____

_____

improving the environment: _____

_____

with great enthusiasm: _____

_____

putting words into practice: _____

_____

reflecting on what had been said: _____

_____

3. Words have the power to lead to good or to bad, and depending on the words we use, we can give good advice or bad advice to others. Place a "G" in front of the expressions below which are good advice and a "B" in front of those which are bad advice.

_____ We should be united and never fight.

_____ If you need it, take it. So what if the owner minds.

_____ Don't backbite.

_____ We all feel lazy once in a while; when you have one of those days, it's better not to do anything.

_____ Don't put off until tomorrow what you can do today.

_____ It doesn't matter if you go to meetings a little late.

_____ No matter how small the task, it should be done with excellence.

_____ It is all right to tell a little white lie every once in a while.

_____ Don't do anything for anybody; it doesn't pay.

_____ The only purpose of life is to have fun.

_____ We should make daily effort to improve ourselves.

_____ Work is punishment.

_____ Why should we obey the law; we all know what is best for ourselves.

_____ Our purpose in this world is to know and to worship God.

_____ We are worshipping God when we do our work in the spirit of service.

_____ We should each worry about our own life and not be bothered by other people's problems.

_____ Your parents are old; what do they know about life today!

_____ A little alcoholic drink every once in a while never hurt anyone.

_____ Life is short. Why kill yourself working!

1. The lesson seeks to expand the consciousness of junior youth by helping them reflect on the concept of the "word". How does it achieve this? _____

_____

_____

_____

_____

_____

_____

_____

_____

2. Having examined the above lesson, what kind of connections can you perceive between the power of thought and the power of utterance? _____

_____

_____

_____

_____

_____

_____

_____

_____

# SECTION 11

Junior youth need to develop the ability to read with ease and to understand well the meaning of what they read. In most parts of the world, there is a diverse range of literature for this age, from academic textbooks to comic magazines. While many elements of this vast body of literature are conducive to the sound development of junior youth, their effect cannot compare with the influence that the truths found in the writings exert on the soul of a youngster. We know that, in this Dispensation, Bahá'u'lláh has endowed every word in His Revelation with a fresh potency. He states:

"Through the movement of Our Pen of glory We have, at the bidding of the omnipotent Ordainer, breathed a new life into every human frame, and instilled into every word a fresh potency. All created things proclaim the evidences of this worldwide regeneration." [24]

Whatever themes or concepts are treated in materials used to develop the powers of expression in junior youth, the meaning conveyed should reflect closely the writings of the Faith. Our understanding of the concept of justice, for instance, if illumined by Bahá'u'lláh's teachings, would penetrate depths of meaning not so accessible in a world that has lost touch with spiritual reality. Discovering the gems of wisdom contained in the writings, with the aid of educational materials imaginatively elaborated, motivates junior youth and creates joy in their hearts. 'Abdu'l-Bahá explains:

"May your souls be illumined by the light of the Words of God, and may you become repositories of the mysteries of God, for no comfort is greater and no happiness is sweeter than spiritual comprehension of the divine teachings. If a man understands the real meaning of a poet's verses such as those of Shakespeare, he is pleased and rejoiced. How much greater his joy and pleasure when he perceives the reality of the Holy Scriptures and becomes informed of the mysteries of the Kingdom!" [25]

The extracts below have been taken from the book *Drawing on the Power of the Word*. The theme of "progress" runs through the entire text. The material strives to assist young minds in gaining an understanding of the concept of progress that is in accord with the teachings of the Faith. You are asked to try to identify the differences between the meaning of progress, say, as conveyed in mass media today and its significance as expressed in the following extracts:

> Some time ago, the people of the village received a visit from a respected teacher who told them, "Alegrías can become a model community, where we can achieve both material and spiritual progress." At the beginning, Diego did not exactly understand what "material and spiritual progress" meant, but he shared the excitement of his entire community. Since then, he has learned a great deal about this matter. He has become aware that, although physically small, he is no longer a child and is capable of helping his village achieve the desired material and spiritual progress.

> It was during one of these conversations that Diego decided to ask everyone what they thought of material and spiritual progress. Mariela, who always has something interesting to say, answered immediately: "I know exactly what material progress means. It means we are poor and we need more money to be able to get the things that will make us happy."

Mariela's comment excited everyone, and they all began to share their opinions. This is more or less what they said:

Antonio:    "I don't believe that to be happy you have to be rich. I know many poor people who are happy."

Carlota:    "My brother is on vacation from the university, and he says that the rich invented the idea of 'the happy poor' to keep us content working for them."

Ana Maria:  "That may be true, but I know that happiness comes from inside and does not depend on how many things a person owns."

Diego:      "But still, it sure isn't much fun to be poor. We should do our best to improve our lives."

Antonio:    "But we should be happy while we are trying to do this. I want to work hard for myself and for my community, but I also want to feel happy doing it. I used to enjoy spending time with Carlota's brother, but ever since he started talking about the rich and the poor I don't like to listen to him. He's so full of anger."

Roberto:    "I know that real happiness comes from being close to God and from obedience to His laws."

Diego:      "That's true, but we can't forget that to love God we should love our fellow human beings and help them."

Carlota:    "And we should remember that obeying the laws of God also means working together to build a better world where people will not be poor anymore."

Then, all of a sudden, Diego realized that so far they had spoken mostly about material progress. "What happened to spiritual progress?" he asked. But everyone was already tired, and they decided to continue the discussion the next time.

The youth dedicated several meetings to the discussion of material and spiritual progress. One month later, just before Elisa's visit, they arranged a special meeting to go over their conclusions. When the youth presented their ideas to Elisa, she was delighted. She helped them to organize their conclusions clearly and to write the following declaration:

## Youth Declaration

We are no longer children and should seriously think about our future. The world in which we live is filled with suffering and afflicted with disunity. We want to build a new world where people live in harmony and where war and poverty no longer exist. In order to build a new world we should begin with our own community. That is why we now speak about material and spiritual progress in our small village, Alegrías. To progress materially, we should improve our agriculture, take better care of our health, have more schools and be active in business and industry. With the fruits of our labors, we should turn our homes, our village and our surroundings into places of great beauty, where we can all enjoy a clean and sanitary environment.

Material progress for all people is not attainable if we do not achieve spiritual progress. Without spirituality, a few become rich while the rest continue to live in poverty. To reach our goals as a community we should be united, act with justice, cooperate and be friendly with one another, and be generous, honest and trustworthy. Justice, generosity, love and kindness, honesty and trustworthiness are spiritual qualities through which we achieve both material and spiritual progress.

It is not only to build a better world that we need spiritual qualities. We also need them for the life of our soul, which does not end on this earth. Material and spiritual progress means that each day we strive for excellence in the material and spiritual aspects of our lives, that we work hard to build a just and peaceful world, and that we prepare ourselves for an eternal life of joy and happiness.

Diego had spent many hours thinking about his speech. Naturally, "The Material and Spiritual Progress of Alegrías" was the subject he wished to address. Yet, he did not want to give a heavy talk on the subject, and he did not want to preach to his friends. So this is the way he went about expressing his ideas:

Being part of the Alegrías youth group has meant a lot to me. Its members are the best friends I have ever had, and some of my happiest moments are when I am with them. I think we have all changed since we began meeting and doing things together. We were more or less children when we started, and our coming together has helped us enter the next stage of our lives in a meaningful way. Thanks to our activities and discussions, we are not entering the stage of youth in a state of confusion and hopelessness. We know we have a purpose in life, and we will help one another achieve our goals. I think we will be friends forever.

One of the ideas we have thought about often since we formed our group is the spiritual and material progress of Alegrías. I think at the beginning we were just curious about what it meant. But now, for most of us, the progress of our community is something to which we wish to dedicate our energies. We hope that our enthusiasm is contagious and will affect everyone in the village.

Thanks to Elisa, who has lovingly guided us, we know some important things about progress. We know that we should always be united, otherwise all our efforts will be wasted. We know we should strive for excellence; every day should be better than the day before. We also know that enlightened words and pure deeds have the power to bring about change. But why do words have such power? One of the most important reasons is that through them we discover, gain and communicate knowledge. At the heart of progress is knowledge.

The other day I was looking at some cows grazing in the pasture near my house. I thought to myself, "These cows have everything they need. All the grass they could possibly desire is there for them to eat. There is a creek that runs through the pasture, from which they can drink whenever they wish. They can lie under the sun or in the shade whenever they want. What more do they need?" But then I realized that that is all they have. They don't have knowledge or understand what they are doing. They are slaves to nature. I decided that I definitely did not want to live like a cow. Then I said to myself, "What if I become extremely wealthy and powerful but remain ignorant? What good will that do? With all that wealth and power I will be nothing but a slave—a slave to my own passions which will drive me to do things I don't even understand, a slave to greed, a slave to others who are wealthier than me and more powerful." That is why knowledge is at the heart of progress. Knowledge gives us freedom.

In the space below, write a few paragraphs describing what you think junior youth should understand about the theme of progress and why.

_____

_____

_____

_____

_____

_____

_____

_____

_____

_____

_____

_____

_____

_____

_____

_____

_____

_____

_____

_____

_____

_____

_____

_____

_____

_____

_____

_____

_____

_____

_____

_____

_____

_____

_____

_____

_____

## SECTION 12

In the writings of the Faith, "utterance" is often qualified by terms such as "crystal clear", "eloquent", "penetrating", "impressive", "moderate", "wise", and laden with "excellent meanings". Words possessing these qualities are expected to have such extraordinary effects as "consuming the veil of self and passion" and "quenching the fire of enmity and hatred". Further, words exert influence in accordance with the spiritual qualities of the one who utters them.

> **"Say: Human utterance is an essence which aspireth to exert its influence and needeth moderation. As to its influence, this is conditional upon refinement which in turn is dependent upon hearts which are detached and pure."** [26]

> **"Moreover words and utterances should be both impressive and penetrating. However, no word will be infused with these two qualities unless it be uttered wholly for the sake of God and with due regard unto the exigencies of the occasion and the people."** [27]

> **"I beseech God to cast upon your heads the pearls of His bounty; to ignite in your hearts the fire of His love; to unloose your tongues to utter the most eloquent words and the most wondrous mysteries in the assemblage of the righteous; to make you flowers of the Abhá Paradise and angels of heaven, united in your views and with your thoughts harmonized; and to manifest in your faces the holy signs of His Kingdom amidst all people."** [28]

> **"If thou wishest thy speech and utterance to penetrate hearts that are hardened, rid thyself of all attachment to the world and turn thy face unto the Kingdom of God."** [29]

1.	Identify from the above passages some of the spiritual qualities that endow human speech with power. _____

_____

_____

_____

2.	How do you think participation in the spiritual empowerment program can contribute to the development of these qualities in junior youth? _____

_____

_____

_____

## SECTION 13

In the writings we are told that the power of speech should be directed towards the realization of lofty goals:

> **"Now is the moment in which to cleanse thyself with the waters of detachment that have flowed out from the Supreme Pen, and to ponder, wholly for the sake of God, those things which, time and again, have been sent down or manifested, and then to strive, as much as lieth in thee, to quench, through the power of wisdom and the force of thy utterance, the fire of enmity and hatred which smoldereth in the hearts of the peoples of the world."** [30]

> **"This servant appealeth to every diligent and enterprising soul to exert his utmost endeavor and arise to rehabilitate the conditions in all regions and to quicken the dead with the living waters of wisdom and utterance, by virtue of the love he cherisheth for God, the One, the Peerless, the Almighty, the Beneficent."** [31]

> **"Every word is endowed with a spirit, therefore the speaker or expounder should carefully deliver his words at the appropriate time and place, for the impression which each word maketh is clearly evident and perceptible. The Great Being saith: One word may be likened unto fire, another unto light, and the influence which both exert is manifest in the world. Therefore an enlightened man of wisdom should primarily speak with words as mild as milk, that the children of men may be nurtured and edified thereby and may attain the ultimate goal of human existence which is the station of true understanding and nobility. And likewise He saith: One word is like unto springtime causing the tender saplings of the rose-garden of knowledge to become verdant and flourishing, while another word is even as a deadly poison. It behooveth a prudent man of wisdom to speak with utmost leniency and forbearance so that the sweetness of his words may induce everyone to attain that which befitteth man's station."** [32]

1. Decide whether the following statements are true or false. The power of expression should be directed towards

    a.  winning an argument.                                          T ☐   F ☐

    b.  expounding the truth by putting forth clear arguments.    T ☐   F ☐

    c.  extinguishing the fire of enmity and hatred in the hearts of people.    T ☐   F ☐

    d.  manipulating others.    T ☐   F ☐

    e.  hiding the truth.    T ☐   F ☐

    f.  explaining the mysteries of the universe.    T ☐   F ☐

    g.  illustrating complex matters.    T ☐   F ☐

    h.  clarifying misunderstandings and building unity of vision.    T ☐   F ☐

    i.  demonstrating the superiority of one's opinions.    T ☐   F ☐

    j.  investigating reality.    T ☐   F ☐

    k.  improving the conditions of the people.    T ☐   F ☐

    l.  defending the rights of the oppressed.    T ☐   F ☐

2. Say a few words about how developing powers of expression assists junior youth on the path of personal transformation as well as in efforts to contribute to the transformation of society.

_____

_____

_____

_____

_____

_____

# SECTION 14

In helping junior youth to develop the powers of expression, we should never forget that it is the Word of God that infuses human speech with power and that endows the human heart and mind with true understanding. Though you are well familiar with this theme, you are asked to pause here nevertheless and reflect on the passages below.

"The Daystar of utterance, shining resplendent from the dayspring of divine Revelation, hath so illumined the Scrolls and Tablets that the kingdom of utterance and the exalted dominion of understanding vibrate with joy and ecstasy and shine forth with the splendor of His light." [33]

"Say: We have caused the rivers of Divine utterance to proceed out of Our throne, that the tender herbs of wisdom and understanding may spring forth from the soil of your hearts." [34]

"Through the breaths of Thine utterance the heaven of understanding hath been adorned, and by the effusions of Thy pen every moldering bone hath been quickened." [35]

"It is clear and evident, therefore, that the first bestowal of God is the Word, and its discoverer and recipient is the power of understanding. This Word is the foremost instructor in the school of existence and the revealer of Him Who is the Almighty. All that is seen is visible only through the light of its wisdom. All that is manifest is but a token of its knowledge. All names are but its name, and the beginning and end of all matters must needs depend upon it." [36]

You may wish to memorize the above quotations, if you do not already know them by heart.


# SECTION 15

We live at a time when humanity is facing moral bankruptcy. Standards that have guided human beings for hundreds of years are steadily losing their influence, and the values of a rampant materialism and of an ideology built on extreme relativism and un-bridled individualism are gradually taking their place. Let us think about this phenomenon further before considering its effects on the young.

It is possible to discern in the course of history over the past few centuries humanity's gradual liberation from so many chains that have long oppressed it—from dogmatism, from tyranny, from superstition, to mention a few. Much of what has been accomplished is praiseworthy indeed. Deeply ingrained prejudices have been overcome, laws to administer justice created, and the rights of individuals and groups acknowledged. Unfortunately, this valuable historical movement is now plagued, and increasingly so, by extremes. Moving into center stage are extreme relativism and unbridled individualism, and the existence of absolutes is being pushed aside. To be free to pursue one's personal preferences is regarded as the highest ideal, and the distinction between right and wrong is becoming blurred as a result. Patterns of behavior based on widely differing sets of values are, in more and more places, considered equivalent, and bonds that have traditionally held the members of a community together have all but lost their strength.

In this climate, youth are left without moral guidance and have difficulty separating truth from falsehood. Nothing but the Word of God can awaken the spiritual susceptibilities that enable the human being to make the distinction. 'Abdu'l-Bahá tells us that the Word of God illumines the realm of thought and morals:

**". . . in the spiritual realm of intelligence and idealism there must be a center of illumination, and that center is the everlasting, ever-shining Sun, the Word of God. Its lights are the lights of reality which have shone upon humanity, illumining the realm of thought and morals, conferring the bounties of the divine world upon man."** [37]

To be able to make moral choices, one needs more than a set of rules; an entire moral structure has to be built in the mind and heart of a young person endowed with a strong social purpose—a structure that connects spiritual concepts, patterns of behavior, and the knowledge of consequences and that is held firm by the forces of volition and courage. Such a moral structure seems to be closely related to the structure of language that operates in the mind of the individual. This language, as stated in the previous few sections, should be rich enough to enable young people to recognize the social, cultural, and ideological forces shaping people's values in a disintegrating world and to understand the nature of the spiritual powers needed to transform them.

The intimate connection between the structure of language in which a person expresses thought and the moral structure that governs his or her thoughts and behavior has important implications for the way both language and morality should be taught. The content of materials used to teach language will necessarily vary according to the values of those who prepare them. It can convey a clear moral message, be morally ambivalent, or even cause spiritual harm. The content of moral education, too, can vary according to the conception of morality being propagated. One can identify, for example, volumes of educational material in which moral concepts are presented as a series of virtues, obligations, rules, and facts aimed at improving behavior without due attention to the elements of language and thought that enhance spiritual perception and foster commitment to social transformation. One can also find programs of moral education that simply ask students to discuss their likes and preferences so that, in clarifying these, they will come to understand themselves as individuals and gain mastery over their own selves. Reducing moral education to either of the two approaches is unwarranted. A program dedicated to the spiritual empowerment of junior youth cannot, of course, shy away from a high moral standard, nor can it ignore that which such a standard demands unambiguously from the individual. At the same time, such a program needs to allow, as we noted earlier, for ample discussion and for the gradual clarification of ideas. It needs, however, to go much further. Particularly, it must pay attention to the role of language in the creation of moral structure, and we will think about this role in the next two sections.

# SECTION 16

Materials employed in an educational program concerned with spiritual empowerment must be written in a language that is open and explorative yet guards against the kind of relativism with which moral education has been so afflicted in recent decades.

*Walking the Straight Path* is another Bahá'í-inspired text that forms part of the junior youth program. It is comprised of twenty stories, each related to a moral theme. In most cultures, stories are used as a means of transmitting wisdom from one generation to the next. In this text, some well-known stories have been rewritten so as to remove the ambiguous messages they have traditionally conveyed. Each lesson also incorporates exercises to enhance linguistic skills and abilities so crucial to the sound development of moral structure. The lesson below begins with a fable with which you may be familiar. It has been rewritten with the purpose of fostering a mode of thought and behavior that is in keeping with a clear moral message. Read the lesson and discuss how the message conveyed by the story avoids the perpetuation of false cultural norms.

*The wise are not fooled by flattery. Everyone, of course, is encouraged by praise. But let us remember that longing for praise weakens our judgment.*

A fox once saw a crow fly off with a piece of cheese in his beak. "I must get that cheese," the fox said to himself and so followed the shadow of the bird until he settled on the branch of a tree.

"Good day, my dear friend," said the fox, putting on his best behavior. "You look so beautiful today. Your feathers are glossy and your eyes shine like jewels. Surely, you have an excellent voice as well. Oh! If only I could hear you sing."

These words were like fresh water satisfying the crow's thirst for praise. So he lifted his head with pride and set out to offer a song in honor of his charming friend.

Of course, the moment he opened his beak, the piece of cheese fell. The fox snapped it up before it hit the ground and ran away, while the crow's not so pleasant voice filled the air.

**COMPREHENSION**

Answer the questions below in complete sentences.

1. What did the fox see? _____

    _____

2. What did the crow have in his beak? _____

    _____

3. What did the fox do to get the cheese? _____

    _____

4. Did the crow really have a pleasant voice? _____

    _____

5. Was the fox sincere in his praise of the crow? _____

_____

6. Did this story occur in a city, village, or forest? _____

_____

**VOCABULARY**

Complete each of the sentences below using one of the following words:

encouraged, longing, charming,
shadow, praise, satisfied, pride,
pleasant, judgment, weakened

1. The teacher thought her students were hardworking and was always full
   of _____ for them.

2. Armando and his brother spent a _____ day
   together, working in the fields and talking about their future plans.

3. Hong Mei liked to travel and had a _____ to see new places.

4. She had a beautiful voice, and her teacher _____ her to
   study music.

5. The farmer showed good _____ in planting his
   seeds right after the first rainfall.

6. Chandu was not _____ with the mark he received
   on his examination, so he decided to study harder.

7. Zhong Jiang was in trouble, but because he had too much _____ ,
   he would not let anyone help him.

8. At the end of the day, the long _____ of the tree falls
   over the garden.

9. It was a _____ story, and the children wanted to listen
   to it again and again.

10. He was greatly _____ by the illness but soon began
    to work again, knowing that he would become stronger in time.

Discuss the following questions in your group:

1.  If one is not careful, this story can be told—indeed, has been told—in a way that implies admiration for the apparent cleverness of the fox. How does the above version of the story avoid giving such an impression? _____

_____

_____

_____

_____

2.  What is the moral message of the story? _____

_____

3.  What are some of the concepts associated with the message? _____

_____

_____

4.  How effective a tool is a fable such as this one in helping junior youth to understand moral concepts? _____

_____

_____

_____

_____

5.  What abilities do the exercises develop in junior youth? _____

_____

_____

_____

_____

_____

6.  How does the discussion exercise contribute to the development of the power of thought and reflection? How does it enhance the powers of expression? _____

_____

_____

_____

_____

_____

7.  How does the memorization of the quotation at the end of the lesson help strengthen these powers? _____

_____

_____

# SECTION 17

If junior youth are to be assisted in recognizing the moral issues underlying the choices they make, it is important to present them with situations that are close to their reality. This does not mean, however, that, in the name of being realistic, attention is drawn to the manifestations of the lower nature of the human being. The situations examined, while accessible to junior youth, need not be the most common in a decaying society but should represent, instead, those standards of thought and conduct that would inspire them to strive for excellence. To this end, materials used in a program for their spiritual empowerment must avoid paternalistic attitudes and childish chatter, on the one hand, and the language of sermons on good behavior, on the other. Consider the following lesson from another Bahá'í-inspired text called *Learning About Excellence*. In the lesson, Mrs. Chen is describing the concept of purity to her grandchildren and assisting them, with the aid of a few exercises, in gaining a fuller grasp of its significance.

Mrs. Chen mentions that the second condition of excellence is a chaste and holy life, which implies modesty, purity, temperance, decency, and clean-mindedness. She begins by describing purity, the foundation on which a chaste life must be built:

"Picture a mirror. If you clean it of all dust, it reflects the light. In the same way, when a heart is cleansed of such imperfections as envy, hate, and pride, it becomes pure and can reflect heavenly light. Mencius has said that the noble man does not lose his childlike heart. This is true of course, but we must remember that a child's heart is pure out of innocence and weakness and that a child's purity has not yet been tested. You are now at an age when you cannot be considered children anymore. As you grow up, you will become wise and strong. Yet, you will each have to be watchful and take great care not to lose the purity of your heart. You should not allow the mirror of your heart to become stained with the impurities of this world. But this you should do through the power of reason and faith. You can remain pure only through effort and the exercise of will."

Mrs. Chen then explains that the concept of purity is often misunderstood and asks her youthful grandchildren to identify from the list below those attributes that imply purity and those that are wrongly associated with it:

Being genuine

Being sincere

Being naive

Being free from hypocrisy

Having a clean mind

Having a clean body

Being stupid

Being free from pride

Being fanatical

Being simpleminded

Being free from deceit

Being selfless

Being weak

Being emotional

Being intelligent

Being kind

Not being pretentious

The youth memorize the quotations below and discuss with their grandparents the questions that follow:

**"My first counsel is this: Possess a pure, kindly and radiant heart, that thine may be a sovereignty ancient, imperishable and everlasting."**

> "First in a human being's way of life must be purity, then freshness, cleanliness, and independence of spirit. First must the stream bed be cleansed, then may the sweet river waters be led into it."

1. A hypocrite is one who pretends to be upright when he is not. What is worse, having many weaknesses or being a hypocrite?

2. What are some of the impurities from which we should cleanse our thoughts?

3. Who actually accomplishes more in this world, the pure in heart or the insincere?

Discuss in your group the following questions:

1. How does the lesson help dissipate common misunderstandings about the concept of purity? _____

_____

_____

_____

2. What are some of the characteristics of the language that is used by Mrs. Chen?

_____

_____

_____

_____

3. How does this lesson help junior youth to strive for spiritual excellence?_____

_____

_____

_____

_____

# SECTION 18

In the last two sections we have considered, if only briefly, the role of language in the creation of moral structure. Our examination of two lessons, one from *Walking the Straight Path* and the other from *Learning About Excellence,* has helped us to see how the discussion of certain themes and concepts, in combination with exercises designed to enhance language skills and abilities, can strengthen patterns of thought conducive to sound moral choices. However important it is to increase language proficiency in this way, we should remember that an individual's moral structure depends on many interacting factors. Specifically, it is difficult to separate the patterns of thinking under discussion here from scientific thinking. Young people need to be prepared to approach the investigation of reality in a scientific manner. A number of the texts they will study, then, will enter into the areas of mathematics and science—not in an effort to teach them as subjects but to strengthen the kind of rationality they engender. In courses that branch off from this book, intended for those who wish to dedicate themselves to working with junior youth over an extended period of several years, these texts will be discussed at some length. For now, it is sufficient for you to simply be aware of this element of the educational process in which the junior youth will engage.

# SECTION 19

Developing spiritual perception, enhancing the powers of expression, and building a sound moral structure are all vital to a process of spiritual empowerment. Unfortunately, to possess power is often associated with values that contradict the spiritual nature of the human being. Images that usually come to mind when the concept is introduced are those of control, manipulation, domination, rule, supremacy, and subjugation. Your aim, however, is to assist junior youth in drawing on a power of a different kind. Moral power springs from love, justice, knowledge, understanding, keen perception, service and, above all, humility. Indeed, humility is a necessary condition of the process of empowerment we are considering here, for it is only through assistance from on High that a gnat can become an eagle, a drop of water be transformed into rivers and seas, and an atom into lights and suns. Reflecting on excerpts from prayers revealed by Bahá'u'lláh and 'Abdu'l-Bahá, in which we supplicate God to grant us certain qualities and attributes, gives us insight into the nature of spiritual and moral empowerment:

> "I pray Thee, O Thou Who art the Lord of all names and the Ruler of both earth and heaven, to grant that all who are dear to Thee may each become a cup of Thy mercy in Thy days, that they may quicken the hearts of Thy servants. Empower them also, O my God, to be as the rain that poureth down from the clouds of Thy grace, and as the winds that waft the vernal fragrances of Thy loving-kindness, that through them the soil of the hearts of Thy creatures may be clad with verdure, and may bring forth the things that will shed their fragrance over all Thy dominion, so that every one may perceive the sweet smell of the Robe of Thy Revelation." [38]

> "Empower us, then, O my God, to spread abroad Thy signs among Thy creatures, and to guard Thy Faith in Thy realm." [39]

> "Empower me, then, O my God, to be reckoned among them that have clung to Thy laws and precepts for the sake of Thee alone, their eyes fixed on Thy face." [40]

> "Empower us, then, O my God, to forsake ourselves and cleave steadfastly to Him Who is the Manifestation of Thy Self, the Most Exalted, the Most High." [41]

"I entreat Thee, by Him Who is the Dayspring of Thy names and the Dawning-Place of Thine attributes, to ordain for me what will enable me to arise to serve Thee and to extol Thy virtues." [42]

"Enable me to be one of Thy maidservants who have attained to Thy good pleasure." [43]

"Protect these children, graciously assist them to be educated and enable them to render service to the world of humanity." [44]

"Send down, then, upon me, O my Beloved, that which will enable me to be steadfast in Thy Cause, so that the doubts of the infidels may not hinder me from turning towards Thee." [45]

"Enable me, then, to obtain a seat of truth in Thy presence, bestow upon me a token of Thy mercy and let me join with such of Thy servants as shall have no fear nor shall they be put to grief." [46]

"O my God, aid Thou Thy servant to raise up the Word, and to refute what is vain and false, to establish the truth, to spread the sacred verses abroad, reveal the splendors, and make the morning's light to dawn in the hearts of the righteous." [47]

"Enable them to distinguish themselves amongst Thy people, that they may exalt Thy word and promote Thy Cause. Aid them, O my God, to do Thy will and pleasure." [48]

# SECTION 20

With our discussion over the past several sections in mind—our examination into the nature of spiritual perception, so imperative to an understanding of reality; our exploration into the powers of expression, so vital to the achievement of lofty goals; our analysis of the relationship between language and moral structure, so crucial in making choices; and our reflections on the process of moral empowerment—let us now consider in some detail two of the books studied by junior youth. In this and the next section we will look at *Breezes of Confirmation,* and in Sections 22 and 23 we will examine *Spirit of Faith.* Both are generally among the first few texts taken up for study by groups in the spiritual empowerment program.

The Bahá'í-inspired text *Breezes of Confirmation* tells the story of Musonda, a young girl who has just turned thirteen, and her older cousin Rose, who has come to visit for the school holidays. Together with Musonda's brother Godwin and his friend Chishimba, the girls think about their future and discuss their hopes and possibilities. There are a number of ideas you will need to explore in your group related to this book. First, however, you are encouraged to read through it once and then again more carefully, carrying out the exercises. After you have done so, you may proceed with the review that follows.

As you have no doubt noticed, the theme that runs through the text is "confirmation". Below are those passages in the book which address the theme, either through discussion among the main characters in the story or through events that demonstrate divine confirmation at work. The passages, each extracted from one of the lessons, are presented in the order they appear in the book. Describe in the spaces provided how the concept of confirmation is treated in each and how you think the junior youth's understanding of it will develop as they go through the lessons.

> "I think about service. I want to do something that can help other people. I would like to become a nurse, but you have to study hard. It also costs and I don't think my parents have enough money," Musonda explains.
>
> "Yes, but you can try, Musonda," says Rose. "There is a word, 'confirmation', that I learned a few weeks ago in one of my classes. My teacher says that God confirms us and helps us in what we do. I like this word very much now. I'm sure you will receive God's confirmation if you set your heart on becoming a nurse."

_____

_____

_____

_____

_____

> Later that night when the girls are in bed, Musonda whispers to Rose, "Rose, you said the word 'confirmation'. Does that mean that if I do the best I can in my schoolwork, God will send us money so that I can study nursing?"
>
> Rose rolls over and looks at Musonda. "Well, not exactly. I mean, I don't know. We have to try things and see what doors open. But I do know that God gives each of us talents. We must find out what our talents are and then learn how to use them," answers Rose.

_____

_____

_____

_____

_____

Godwin has a classmate and a close friend whose name is Chishimba. He often visits the Mulengas, and tonight he is staying for dinner. The conversation at the table jumps from one subject to another. Musonda wants to bring up the subject of confirmation, and she is impatient. Finally, there are a few moments of silence. "Rose and I have been talking about confirmation," says Musonda.

"There goes my little sister," says Godwin, clearing his throat. But to his surprise, Chishimba looks interested.

"What does the word mean to you?" he asks Musonda.

Musonda, also surprised, looks at Rose, hoping that she will answer.

"Confirmation . . . God confirms us and helps us in what we do," says Rose.

Chishimba does not say anything for a while. There is sadness in his eyes. "A few months ago," he slowly begins, "my father lost his job. He is honest and responsible, and everyone knows it. For eighteen years he worked as a guard in a company, and then, all of a sudden, they fired him. We all know the reason. If they had kept him two more years, he would have retired and the company would have had to pay him his pension. We don't have a lot of savings. Even though my older brother helps us, it looks like I cannot go back to school next year because I cannot pay for my room and board. I really love school. I wonder why God does not help me."

Everyone looks in the direction of Mr. Mulenga, expecting him to answer this question.

Mr. Mulenga smiles and says, "That God confirms us when we make an effort does not mean that life is easy. Your lives will be full of difficulties, and unfortunately, many of them will be caused by injustice. But you will have to work hard, and even though things may not go the way you wish for a while, you should be sure of God's confirmation. He will especially confirm you in your efforts to do away with injustice." He turns to Chishimba and says, "Your family is united and hardworking. My heart tells me that things will change for you. You will finish your studies. Take my word for it."

_____

_____

_____

_____

_____

_____

The following Monday the two girls go with Mrs. Phiri to the clinic. When the time comes for the mothers to begin their class, Musonda and Rose take the children outside and sit with them in the shade of a tree. They sing songs and play games together, and Rose tells them a story. Just as the story is ending, the mothers arrive to pick up their children. Everyone is happy. Mrs. Phiri and the other health workers are pleased and ask the girls to come back the next week.

On their way home, Musonda is very thoughtful. Finally she breaks the silence and says to Rose, "Do you think that what happened today has something to do with 'confirmation'? You want to be a teacher and I want to be a nurse, and here we were in a clinic teaching and taking care of children."

_____

_____

_____

_____

_____

In the weeks since Rose has come to be with her, the two girls have talked about many things, and Musonda's head is full of ideas. So one morning she decides to go to her favorite place. As she lies on the rock, she remembers the day at the clinic. "It was good to do something useful," she thinks to herself. She remembers what her father often says, that trees should bear fruit. Then she wonders, "How will I make sure that my life bears good fruits?" She thinks immediately of the word "confirmation".

Just then there is a strong gust of wind. It blows some leaves into the air. Among the leaves Musonda sees a small yellow bird. After the wind dies down, the leaves all fall into the water, but the bird continues flying. As she watches the bird, a thought comes to her mind. The wind has given the little bird a push, and now it is flying higher and higher. Maybe that is what confirmation means. The bird made the effort to fly and the wind helped it.

_____

_____

_____

_____

_____

_____

_____

"Do you think about your future, Godwin?" Musonda asks. "What do you want to be?"

Godwin continues working on the bicycle. "I don't know. I want to make money. I want to help our parents and have a family someday," he answers.

"But do you ever think about your talents and how you can use them?" asks Musonda. "Rose and I talk about this a lot."

"I know, I know," he says as he picks up a wrench. "And you *always* talk about 'confirmation' . . . 'God helps us when we make an effort.'"

"But Godwin, it is true." Then she tells him the story of the yellow bird and the wind. She also tells him about the work she and Rose have been doing with the children at the clinic.

Just then Chishimba arrives. "Hello," he says. "How is the bicycle? Did you figure out the problem?" he asks.

"The problem was in the gears. I'm still working on it," answers Godwin as he tightens a bolt.

"I knew you could fix it!" Chishimba says, and then looks at Musonda. "Do you know that your brother is a mechanic?"

Rose comes out of the house and hears part of the conversation. "Godwin," she says, "that is one of your talents! You are good at fixing things. You could be a good mechanic!"

"Just because I can fix a bicycle," Godwin says, "does not mean I am a mechanic. I would need training."

The other three smile and say, "So, make an effort!" Everyone laughs, even Godwin.

"Godwin, why don't you talk to Mr. Chiyesu, the mechanic with the shop near the market? Maybe he would teach you," says Chishimba with excitement in his voice.

"Yes, that could be a way to start," adds Rose.

"What?" asks Godwin. "I can't just go and ask him like that. I don't even know him."

"I know him. I can introduce you. We can go together tomorrow," says Chishimba.

Later, when they are alone, Rose says to Musonda, "Tomorrow Godwin will understand the meaning of confirmation." They laugh, but decide not to say anything to the boys.

Mr. Chiyesu, a short, elderly man, is sitting outside of his shop. He is cleaning the pieces of a small engine and humming a melody while he works. His face lights up when he sees Chishimba, and they shake hands.

Chishimba introduces Godwin and explains that he is good at fixing things. Godwin is nervous, but he finds the courage to speak up. He clears his throat and says, "Mr. Chiyesu, I am interested in becoming a mechanic. So I was thinking maybe I could help you in your shop and learn from you."

"Well, I could use the help," responds Mr. Chiyesu. "But, I don't have the money to pay you."

"It does not matter. I just want to learn," says Godwin. "When can I start?"

"There's no time better than now!" answers Mr. Chiyesu. "Can you stay this morning? These pieces need oiling, and then we have to put the engine back together."

"Now? I can start right now?" asks Godwin with surprise.

"Of course!" laughs Mr. Chiyesu. "Roll up your sleeves and get working!"

Godwin eagerly begins his new work. After a few minutes Chishimba stands up to leave. He says goodbye to Mr. Chiyesu. He leans over and whispers "confirmation" in Godwin's ear.

On his way home, Chishimba passes the clinic and sees Rose and Musonda helping with the children. The girls are curious to know what happened. "How did it go?" they ask.

"Godwin made an effort and it worked. He is there right now. I think Mr. Chiyesu wanted to test him out," answers Chishimba.

_____

_____

_____

_____

_____

_____

_____

_____

_____

_____

_____

_____

One morning Chishimba is on his way to the market to buy fish for his mother. He has been thinking for days about how to earn money for school. He thought of growing a crop to sell, but the planting season is over. He thought about selling charcoal at the roadside, but many people are doing this. "Try to do something that no one else is doing," he remembers Rose saying.

When he arrives at Mrs. Musole's stand to buy the fish, he finds out that she is not there. "She went to town to bring the fish," says the woman in the next stand. "She goes twice a week." Chishimba knows that Mr. Chiyesu also goes to town sometimes to buy car parts.

This gives him an idea. "Maybe I could offer to go to town for people," he thinks to himself, "and bring the things they need. By staying and working then, they would not lose money."

That night at home Chishimba consults with his parents, and they like the idea. So the next day he returns to the market and talks with Mrs. Musole and Mr. Chiyesu. "If you both pay me the money you would normally spend on bus fare, I will use half of it to go to town and bring you what you need. The other half I will save for school." They agree that it is worth a try and ask him to come back in two days. "If this idea works well," says Mr. Chiyesu, "then you have found yourself a job!"

On his way home to tell his parents the good news, Chishimba stops to see Godwin and his family. He is eager to share his plan with them. After listening to his story, Mrs. Mulenga gives Chishimba some more good news. She explains that Mr. Mulenga had to go to Kabwe the day before and spoke to her cousin. He said that Chishimba was welcome to stay with him and his family, about one kilometer from the school. "In exchange for meals and a place to sleep," she says, "you can help in their fields."

"That is great!" says Chishimba. "Thank you, Mrs. Mulenga."

"Chishimba," says Mr. Mulenga, "It seems that you will soon be making some money. You will have to make sure that you save it for school, even though sometimes that may seem difficult. Don't be tempted to spend it on silly little things."

"Don't worry, Mr. Mulenga," replies Chishimba, his face beaming with a smile. "I promise I will not let that happen." As he waves goodbye and turns to leave, he looks over at Rose and Musonda and says, "Doors are opening!"

_____

_____

_____

_____

_____

_____

_____

_____

The holidays are coming to an end. It is time for Rose to go home and start school again. As she prepares to leave, she and Musonda talk.

"I wish you did not have to go," says Musonda.

"Me, too," says Rose. "It was really a wonderful holiday. I cannot believe all the things that have happened."

"Yes," says Musonda. "Look at Godwin. He liked his job so much that now he is talking about getting technical training after he finishes school. And Chishimba's idea really worked well. He ended up with so many clients that he was going into town almost every day."

"And look at us," says Rose. "Working at the health clinic was a great experience. I am even more convinced that I want to be a teacher. My village council arranges weekly classes for children of different ages, and almost all the children go. This year I plan to offer to teach one of the classes."

"And I will try to keep working at the clinic," says Musonda. "I can't go on Mondays anymore because of school, but maybe I can help out some afternoons. You know, Rose, that first day we talked about 'confirmation', I couldn't have imagined how important it was and how understanding it would change our lives."

"It is true," agrees Rose. "Look at how much we have all changed because we learned about making effort and expecting confirmations."

_____

_____

_____

_____

_____

_____

_____

_____

_____

On the way back home, Musonda asks if she can go down by the river. She runs to her special place, climbs on the rock and lies on her back, looking up at the sky. Many thoughts are going through her mind. She thinks about the school holidays and wonders what the coming year will bring. It is a windy day, and she remembers the yellow bird. "Whatever I try," she whispers to herself, "God will help me." As she gets up to leave, the wind blows against her back and gives her strength.

_____

_____

_____

_____

_____

_____

_____

_____

# SECTION 21

In general, being well familiar with the content of the books—in this case, *Breezes of Confirmation*—and having a good understanding of how they try to accomplish their aims will enable you to assume your responsibilities as the animator of a junior youth group with confidence. In addition, you need to reflect on the methods you will use to assist the group in studying the books and in benefiting from what they offer. The skills and abilities you require for this purpose will, of course, develop gradually as you gain experience, but the following exercises, related specifically to *Breezes of Confirmation,* will provide you with many insights in this respect.

1.   The readings in the book try to maintain a certain level of simplicity in terms of sentence structure and flow. However, where needed, difficult words and phrases are readily employed. The lessons draw out the meaning of such words by placing them in different contexts and through the use of exercises. By allowing for a rich vocabulary in this way, the story avoids the tendency of becoming childish and superficial. Injustice, for example, is a complex concept, although the word is used often in everyday speech. The context in which it is introduced in Lesson 6 and the corresponding exercises assist junior youth in gaining some grasp of the concept. Do you find this approach effective for young people in early adolescence, or do you think it is necessary for you to go through every lesson and define "difficult" words for them?

_____

_____

_____

_____

_____

2.   The lessons of this book were written to be studied at a sprightly pace, in an atmosphere of joy and thoughtful reflection. It is assumed that the youth will read the story and carry out the exercises more or less quickly. What would happen if you tried to accomplish more than the intended goal of each lesson and belabored every point it makes?

_____

_____

_____

_____

_____

3.   The attention span of junior youth is not short, as is often assumed. While maintaining the ability to enjoy the simple things of life, they are also able to think deeply about ideas that challenge them. If the atmosphere of the group is one of trust, free from the kind of tension that permeates classrooms in so many schools

of the world, reflection will occur naturally and will begin and end according to the needs and capacities of the junior youth in each group. What steps can you take to create the desired atmosphere?

_____

_____

_____

_____

_____

_____

4.	The study of the book does not envision "homework". Exercises are to be done in the meetings of the group and discussed with the help of the animator. How would the nature of the program change by treating group meetings like a class, for example, by leaving the exercises as homework?

_____

_____

_____

_____

_____

_____

5.	Most lessons in this book include an activity in which junior youth are asked to write a few sentences, either about the section of the story they have just studied or about a particular idea and its application to their lives. How would you assist the junior youth in carrying out this type of activity, helping them to develop the ability to express themselves clearly without turning the meeting of the group into a class on writing?

_____

_____

_____

_____

_____

_____

6.	Lessons 2, 5, 9, 10, 13, and 14 of the book each end with a quotation from the writings that the junior youth are encouraged to memorize. You may find it helpful to refer to one or two of these in order to examine how this last activity reinforces the principal concepts being conveyed in the lessons.

_____

_____

7. In addition to the main theme, the book touches on many moral concepts and tries to reinforce praiseworthy qualities and attitudes. Rose, for example, shares her food with a child on the bus. Godwin and Chishimba help a woman carry firewood. Rose and Musonda teach children while their mothers are attending classes on nutrition at the clinic. The football game is a friendly event in which "winning" is not the overarching purpose. How much attention should be given to these points? Should every one of them be identified and considered in detail? Or, is it sufficient to allow them to come up naturally during discussion?

_____

_____

_____

_____

_____

_____

8. The story unfolds in an African village. The books that form part of the junior youth spiritual empowerment program portray reality in a number of cultural and social settings in various continents. This adds to the richness of the program. Some may suggest that there is a need to "adapt the books to the reality of the youth in each country" by, for example, changing the names of the characters in the stories. Yet people have read books from cultures other than their own for centuries, have enjoyed them and learned from them. They have, of course, done so consciously. How would you make the junior youth aware of this dimension of the program? What are your thoughts on the belief held by some that children and youth learn only from materials written in the context of their own culture?

_____

_____

_____

_____

_____

_____

# SECTION 22

*Spirit of Faith*, as we noted earlier, is one of several texts that provide content for the continuation of Bahá'í children's classes and in which explicit reference is made to the Central Figures of the Faith. We have already mentioned before that adolescence is a stage in life when an individual is highly interested in exploring questions of a philosophical character, especially those related to the purpose and nature of human existence. *Spirit of Faith* begins by asking the question, "What does it mean to be a human being?" In trying to answer this question, the various lessons of the book examine a series of related ideas: the nobility of the human being, the higher and lower natures of the human being; the nonexistence of evil; the nature of free will, volition, and fate; the power of the intellect; scientific investigation; physical evolution; the spirit of man; and, finally, the spirit of faith.

As was the case with *Breezes of Confirmation,* you need to go through the book once and then read it again more carefully, this time paying particular attention to the sections referred to as "reflections". After having done so, you should analyze how the book sets out to achieve its purpose by answering the following questions:

1.  Several passages from the Writings of Bahá'u'lláh are quoted in Lesson 1 that contain images which help junior youth think about their true identity. What insight does each image offer in this connection? How does each of the reflections in the lesson reinforce their understanding of the subject? _____

     _____

     _____

     _____

     _____

2.  How do junior youth gain an appreciation of God's creation and the nobility of the human being from the first part of Lesson 2? _____

     _____

     _____

     _____

3.  How does the first reflection of that lesson help them see the application of the concept of nobility in their lives? _____

     _____

     _____

     _____

4.  In the next part of the lesson they think about that which causes people to abase themselves. What is it? _____

     _____

     _____

     _____

5.  What understanding do you hope a junior youth would derive from this brief study of the higher and lower natures of the human being? _____

     _____

     _____

     _____

6. What do junior youth learn about the development of their higher nature through the second reflection of the lesson? _____

_____

_____

_____

7. How does realizing that the lower nature of the human being is not evil help junior youth to avoid feelings of guilt every time they make a mistake? What examples are used to help deepen their understanding of the theme? _____

_____

_____

_____

8. What insights does the latter part of Lesson 2, particularly the final two reflections, offer on how to control the dictates of the lower nature? _____

_____

_____

_____

9. How is the concept of volition treated in Lesson 3? Do you find the situation described at the beginning of the lesson relevant to the lives of young people?

_____

_____

_____

_____

10. What do junior youth learn in Lesson 3 in relation to the role of free will in the development of their higher nature? _____

_____

_____

_____

11. In which areas of their lives do junior youth come to understand that they can exercise free will? Why is it important for them to know the limitations of their free will? _____

_____

_____

_____

12. What further insights do they gain into the operation of their free will from the second reflection in the lesson? _____

_____

_____

_____

13. Why is it important for junior youth to see the difference between controlling others and exerting positive influence on them? How do you think the discussions generated in the third reflection help the junior youth in their efforts to exert a positive influence on their environment? _____

_____

_____

_____

14. What does Lesson 3 teach junior youth about the concept of fate? _____

_____

_____

_____

15. What misconceptions about the nature of fate does the lesson try to remove? ___

_____

_____

_____

16. How effective is the metaphor of the sailboat in helping junior youth gain the proper perspective on the value of their own efforts and the power of divine assistance in their lives? _____

_____

_____

_____

17. In what way does the first part of Lesson 4 help junior youth discover the limitations of nature? _____

_____

_____

_____

18. What does the lesson say about the way human beings transcend these limitations? _____

_____

_____

_____

19. What does the statement that "God has created or deposited this love of reality in man" mean? In what sense does science belong to all humanity? _____

_____

_____

_____

20. How is the power of observation described for the junior youth? _____

_____

_____

_____

21. How does the example provided in Lesson 4 assist junior youth in appreciating the role of observation and experimentation in the advancement of science?

_____

_____

_____

22. Does the lesson imply that they can use their power of observation in every aspect of life? Why do you think the questions asked in the third reflection, which encourages them to exercise this power, all focus on the higher nature of the human being? _____

_____

_____

_____

23. The examples provided in the fourth reflection imply that experimentation cannot be used in every aspect of life. How do they help junior youth appreciate the significance of this principle? _____

_____

_____

_____

24. How do the various examples used in Lessons 5 and 6 help junior youth gain insights into the very complex theory of the evolution of species? _____

_____

_____

_____

25. How is the appearance of the spirit of man described in this evolutionary process? _____

_____

_____

_____

26. In Lesson 6 the animator, Natalia Petrovna, reads two quotations from the Writings of 'Abdu'l-Bahá to the group of junior youth in the story and then helps them to study and understand them. There is no indication of how she does so. How would you go about explaining the quotations? _____

_____

_____

_____

27.   What is the distinguishing feature of the spirit of man as described in the first
      section of Lesson 7? _____

      _____

      _____

      _____

28.   How is consciousness introduced in the first reflection of that lesson? How relevant
      to the lives of junior youth are the two exercises in the reflection? _____

      _____

      _____

      _____

29.   How can the power of the human mind become an instrument of the higher nature?
      Is the presentation of contrasts, as is done in the second reflection, a useful way
      of underscoring the importance of guiding human intellect? _____

      _____

      _____

      _____

30.   What is the spirit of faith? _____

      _____

      _____

      _____

31.   How do the last two reflections of Lesson 7 help junior youth see the operation of
      the spirit of faith in their lives? _____

      _____

      _____

      _____

# SECTION 23

At the heart of the text _Spirit of Faith_ lies the principle of harmony between science
and religion. The implications of this profound principle for the life of humanity will be
the object of your ongoing reflections in the years to come, and you will gain fresh insight
into its operation as you continue to study, to act, and to consult and reflect on experience.
For the sake of consultation here, the statement below on the relationship between science
and religion is being provided, in the hope that it will offer you some fruitful points for
consideration. Read it and then complete the exercises that follow.

*In principle, a number of relationships can exist between religion and science. It can be claimed, for example, that whatever truth is expounded by religion about spiritual phenomena today will one day be explained by science and that religion, a very necessary aspect of human experience, simply gives partial answers to mysteries which will be understood later as science advances. It can also be argued that, since religion is the result of God's Revelation, and God knows everything, religion already contains all scientific truth, albeit in ways that are sometimes difficult to discover. The first view, of course, would be rejected by many a religious person as it seems to minimize the role of God and revelation in the creation of religion. The second view seems to confuse the knowledge available to the Manifestation of God with what we human beings can understand by studying His Revelation.*

*Another possibility is to argue that science and religion are so distinct that there is no possibility of significant conflict between them. Science studies the material universe. The knowledge it generates becomes the basis for technological progress, and technology can be employed either for the good of humanity or to its detriment, for building civilization or for its destruction. Science in itself does not have the ability to determine the uses to which its products should be put. Religion, by contrast, is concerned precisely with the spiritual dimension of human existence. Its task is to throw light on the inner life of the individual, to touch the roots of motivation, to engender a code of ethics and morality that can appropriately guide human behavior. So long as each remains within the sphere of its own genius, there is no reason for them to come into conflict with each other.*

*This view of the harmony between science and religion is valid, but only at the level of application. Ultimately, in this approach, science and religion are separated and allowed to pursue their own ways, and what assumes importance is the interaction between technology and morality. But such an analysis of the relation between science and religion soon reaches its limits, for, in fact, there are numerous phenomena which they both try to understand and explain. While this is less noticeable in relation to nature, it is evident in the study of the human being and society. Moreover, there are many commonalities between science and religion in the way they approach reality. For example, both have faith in the existence of order in creation and believe that, at least to some extent, the human mind is capable of understanding this order. The methods of science have proven extremely effective in discovering the workings of the universe. But religion, too, has to use these methods as it tries to guide human beings to contribute to an ever-advancing civilization. Science and religion are not the same, but they have enough in common to be able to speak to each other, to be in harmony, to influence and to complement one another.*

1.  The relationship between science and religion described in the above statement envisions areas of knowledge which both science and religion explore. Among these are issues related to the powers of the human mind, the origins of the human being, and intellectual and moral development. Discuss how, in treating such matters, *Spirit of Faith* respects the validity of science while at the same time allowing the light of religion to illumine understanding.

_____

_____

_____

_____

2.      The principle of the harmony between science and religion implies that, when
        appropriate, educational materials may integrate spiritual and scientific concepts,
        of course in a manner that avoids superficiality and that is not haphazard. Such
        integration of knowledge enhances understanding and removes false dichotomies.
        Examine how *Spirit of Faith* achieves this level of integration. You may refer
        specifically to reflections in Lessons 5 and 6.

        _____

        _____

        _____

        _____

        _____

3.      You may wish to examine *Spirit of Faith* again and determine the extent to which
        it engenders certain attitudes that are deemed necessary for one who is to be a
        seeker of truth and an investigator of reality. What are some of these attitudes and
        how effectively does the material explore them?

        _____

        _____

        _____

        _____

        _____

        _____

# SECTION 24

We will end here the discussion on which we embarked in Section 3 regarding the
texts studied in the junior youth spiritual empowerment program. The detailed analyses
we have undertaken of *Breezes of Confirmation* and *Spirit of Faith* give an indication of
the degree of familiarity that you will need to reach with every one of the texts in the
program. In courses branching off from Book 5, we will enter into a similar discussion of
other texts, which will assist you in this connection; however, independent of such study,
you should dedicate the necessary time to reading the texts and examining how they strive
to accomplish their aims. Periodic meetings of reflection with others serving as animators
will offer some of the most fruitful opportunities for you to deepen your understanding
of the material. You and your fellow animators will find, on such occasions, a wealth of

shared experience upon which to draw. For, in the final analysis, it is only in the creation of an atmosphere of mutual support and assistance, where the commitment to learning finds expression in a willingness to accompany others in their endeavors, that the potential of the texts can be fully explored and eventually realized.

# SECTION 25

It was mentioned earlier in this unit that the study of material takes only a portion of the time junior youth spend together; the rest is dedicated to service activities, sports, and different forms of cultural expression suited to their particular surroundings. In the second unit of this book, you had an opportunity to consider, to a certain extent, the influence of the social environment on young people, and you were alerted especially to some of its harmful effects. The emphasis given there to the worsening conditions of society today should not be allowed, however, to obscure the fact that there are many elements in every environment which, if used properly, can enhance the powers of expression, the ability to analyze social processes, and the will to serve humanity. The following newspaper article tells a story that illustrates well how the media, for example, can be used to promote the welfare of society:

## Voice of the Voiceless

In West Africa the transistor radio still speaks for the community.

Huddled around a microphone in the tiny studio of Nzérékoré rural radio station in the forest region of Guinea, three young people are discussing girls' education.

"Girls should go to school, because they'll become mothers one day, and if they are educated, they'll educate their own children and will be able to look after them better," says Moriko Kaké. "When you educate a girl, you educate an entire nation," he adds emphatically. Lancei Touré, the program's sixteen-year-old host, nods in agreement, although his parents want him to leave school to work in the fields.

The young people's clear, articulate arguments are broadcast live to neighboring villages near the Liberian and Ivory Coast borders. It is dusk, and kerosene lamps flicker inside mud huts. Villagers are back from the fields or the market. They all listen to the radio while cooking dinner and preparing for the night.

Fifty years ago, the first transistor radio made its way into people's houses, turning a bulky piece of furniture into a cheap, small personal device that can be listened to by anyone, anywhere. . . .

In countries such as Guinea—where a large part of the adult population is illiterate, many children don't have access to school and electricity is rare—generator-powered rural and community radio stations are a lifeline.

"Radio is everything here," says Gnouma Camara, program director at Nzérékoré rural radio station, which broadcasts six days a week in one of five regional languages and in French within a radius of 100km. Two out of three families in the region have a transistor, and when the station broadcasts early in the morning and in the evening, the whole village listens.

"We speak their own language, we know their traditions and customs, we transmit their messages, announce births and deaths, discuss farming and agriculture issues and community problems," Camara adds. "We are the voice of the community. The voice of the voiceless." . . .

"I listen to the programs because it is children who present them and because they speak in my own language," says Mamadou Malic, a fifteen-year-old youth in Pular, a local tongue. . . . "When the programs start, I call all my brothers and sisters and we listen together. I learn a lot that way."

"Parents and community leaders are listening too," says Camara. "In our culture, children are not often heard, but now adults start to listen to them. Children advise their parents on basic hygiene, for example. . . . If a father hits his child, his neighbors will now say: 'Don't you listen to the radio?'"

This story points to only one of the myriad ways in which various elements of the social environment can be drawn upon in directing the talents and abilities of young people towards service to their communities. Music, media, and technology are increasingly affecting the lives of the young in every part of the world. As an animator, you will need to remain conscious of these powerful elements and learn to help junior youth employ them to create appropriate activities. Think about your own social environment. What possibilities does it open to junior youth to work with the following? Discuss your ideas in your group, and write down some of your thoughts in the spaces provided.

Music: _____

_____

_____

_____

_____

Media: _____

_____

_____

_____

_____

Technology: _____

_____

_____

_____

_____

# SECTION 26

If junior youth are to be empowered to take charge of their own development and contribute to the progress of their communities, they need to participate not only in the implementation of meaningful activities as a group but also in their formulation. Special events in which junior youth from an entire region or cluster come together to make dramatic presentations, sing, recite poetry, and give talks; ecological camps in which passages from the writings about the environment are read, appreciation of nature is fostered, and activities such as planting trees are carried out; periodic sessions in which newspaper and magazine articles are discussed and current events analyzed—these are a few examples of the kinds of activity that the youth may find highly stimulating. You will always be interested in discussing with other animators how you can motivate the youth to take part in the design and execution of activities that train their intellectual and spiritual faculties, help them express in practice some of their ideals through service, and reinforce their efforts to strive towards excellence. The types of questions you will need to consider with your fellow animators include the following: How do you help junior youth devise and carry out a service project and reflect on the way it unfolds? How do you select appropriate newspaper articles, and how do you organize discussions about them? How do you help junior youth write scripts and perform simple dramas? How do you ensure that childish games are not presented as a substitute for arts and crafts and that young people are assisted in gaining a true appreciation of "arts, crafts and sciences" that "uplift the world of being, and are conducive to its exaltation"?

The last point deserves further consideration. The question of artistic expression is closely connected to culture, and it is especially for this reason that it is left to individual groups around the world to formulate their own activities. Read the passage below from a letter dated 12 December 2011 written by the Universal House of Justice:

> **"Propelled by forces generated both within and outside the Bahá'í community, the peoples of the earth can be seen to be moving from divergent directions, closer and closer to one another, towards what will be a world civilization so stupendous in character that it would be futile for us to attempt to imagine it today. As this centripetal movement of populations accelerates across the globe, some elements in every culture, not in accord with the teachings of the Faith, will gradually fall away, while others will be reinforced. By the same token, new elements of culture will evolve over time as people hailing from every human group, inspired by the Revelation of Bahá'u'lláh, give expression to patterns of thought and action engendered by His teachings, in part through artistic and literary works. It is with such considerations in mind that we welcome the decision of the Ruhi Institute, in formulating its courses, to leave for the friends to address locally issues related to artistic activity."** [49]

The House of Justice goes on to say:

> **"We long to see, for instance, the emergence of captivating songs from every part of the world, in every language, that will impress upon the consciousness of the young the profound concepts enshrined in the Bahá'í teachings. Yet such an efflorescence of creative thought will fail to materialize, should the friends fall, however inadvertently, into patterns prevalent in the world that give**

license to those with financial resources to impose their cultural perspective on others, inundating them with materials and products aggressively promoted. Further, every effort should be made to protect spiritual education from the perils of commercialization. The Ruhi Institute itself has explicitly discouraged the proliferation of products and items that treat its identity as a brand to be marketed. We hope that the friends will respect its diligence in this matter." [50]

Though this is not the occasion to enter into a discussion of artistic activity, it is important for you to be aware that such activity, as an expression of culture, carries with it values. By its very nature, then, it can influence an educational process greatly. As an animator of a junior youth group, you will want to take care in helping your young friends identify suitable artistic pursuits, ones that do not end up inadvertently imposing values that contradict, in subtle ways, the educational process in which they are engaged.

## SECTION 27

If employed imaginatively, complementary activities can serve to reinforce the lessons being learned by junior youth in their study of the materials. The content of these activities might be either directly based on the texts themselves or merely inspired by them. Though you should not devise such activities on behalf of the junior youth, who will be eager to consult together and arrive at their own conclusions, you may find it helpful, as an exercise, to choose in your group today one of the lessons from *Breezes of Confirmation* and design an activity that reinforces the concepts presented in it.

## SECTION 28

The system of delivery for a program concerned with the spiritual empowerment of junior youth may include regular meetings held over the course of a year, as well as intensive sessions lasting several weeks each. Experience has shown that an animator wishing to start a group can easily begin with one or two junior youth who have shown an ability to rally their friends around a worthy cause. Successful identification of such individuals will naturally lead to the formation of a group composed of ten to fifteen members. In some parts of the world, inviting the young members of a village or neighborhood to a series of events before the formal establishment of groups has also proved to be effective. Another approach is to introduce the program to a school. When the school shows receptivity to the idea, one or more presentations to the students and teachers of the relevant grades usually result in the formation of several junior youth groups. Often the groups are able to meet on school premises and undertake their activities as extracurricular endeavors. The school, in turn, recognizes the valuable contribution of the program to the sound development of the moral and intellectual capabilities of its students.

Think about your own circumstances and describe some of the approaches you could adopt in forming a junior youth group.

_____
_____
_____
_____
_____
_____
_____

# SECTION 29

An important requirement for maintaining a dynamic junior youth group is building trust and friendship with the parents. Animators need to visit parents either before or soon after the formation of groups and explain to them the purpose of the program. They should continue to visit the parents regularly thereafter; explore with them themes central to the lives of junior youth that the program tries to address, as outlined in the second unit of this book; and consult with them about the well-being and progress of their sons and daughters. Often animators will show parents one or two of the texts studied so that they are familiar with what the junior youth are learning. Though generally every animator will need to cultivate such bonds of friendship with parents over an extended period of many months, a more experienced individual may accompany him or her on the first few visits.

In the space below, describe how you would explain the program to the parents of a young person during an initial conversation, and then write down some of the ideas that you would share with them in subsequent visits.

_____
_____
_____
_____
_____
_____
_____
_____
_____
_____
_____
_____
_____

# SECTION 30

It is essential that, in the first few meetings of the group, its purpose be fully discussed, together with a few of the collective goals its members hope to accomplish. The youth should also reach some conclusions about the nature of the activities they wish to undertake. The concepts of excellence and service need to be emphasized. Many experienced animators find that their conversations during the first four meetings are particularly significant. Subjects addressed in these meetings may well vary from group to group. Yet there are a number of ideas that generally run through all such meetings. The following points may assist you, then, in organizing the first conversations you will have with the members of each group you help to form.

- Often the first questions posed by the animator in the initial meeting are "What is the purpose of a junior youth group?" and "Why is it important to have such groups in the community?" If the youth have difficulty answering such general questions, the animator may ask individual members more specific ones, for example, "Why do you like being part of this group?" or "What kinds of things do you think the group should do?" This line of questioning should gradually lead to a list of goals and activities.

- Several animators have found it useful to describe the goals identified by the group in terms of spiritual and intellectual excellence. To strive for spiritual excellence, they have explained, we need to develop qualities that belong to our higher nature such as love, generosity, honesty, and humility. To strive for intellectual excellence, we need to acquire knowledge and practical skills that will help us improve our lives and the lives of others. Reflecting on quotations such as "Let each morn be better than its eve and each morrow richer than its yesterday" and committing them to memory have proved effective in enhancing the understanding of the concept of excellence.

- It is useful for animators to emphasize in the first few meetings that, for the group to strive for spiritual excellence, the members need to develop strong bonds of friendship and achieve greater and greater unity. There are a number of quotations from the writings related to this subject, and several can be selected for the youth to discuss and memorize. Animators find it particularly fruitful to help the youth express their own ideas on the themes of love, unity, and harmony. The concept of friendship usually proves to be appropriate for an initial conversation of this kind.

- A topic of great importance for the early discussions of the group is service. In this respect, the youth should be reminded that, as human beings, we all depend on one another. They can be asked to imagine what it would be like for us if we did not receive help from anyone at all. That we are all members of the human family and must try our best to improve the conditions in which we live should be emphasized in such discussions. One way of making the concept of service accessible to the junior youth is to explain that everything we do in the spirit of helping others can be considered service.

- Discussions of service need to go beyond the question of the individual's efforts to serve others and consider what the youth can do as a group. Of course, it is important that their initial endeavors be of a short duration, with easily achievable goals. In this way, they will gain confidence in their collective capacity and will learn to work together, opening up the possibility for them to undertake more sustained service projects. From the outset, animators should guide the youth in setting in motion a process in which they think about the life of their community and how they can contribute to its betterment. Asking questions that require them to make observation statements about the community will assist them in this connection. Thus, they may begin with an act of service as simple as visiting someone in the community who is sick and gradually move on to undertake a project—for example, planting trees—in which they will need to consult with appropriate local institutions, elicit assistance from friends and parents, and make long-term arrangements. Naturally, during the first few meetings of the group, some of the skills and abilities as well as attitudes and qualities necessary for effective cooperation are discussed.

- Healthy recreation, particularly sports, is another topic that has to be addressed during the first meetings of a junior youth group. Once again, in addition to an examination of the concepts and issues involved, animators will want to help the group identify the kind of recreational activities that can be undertaken either during its meetings or on special occasions. A word of caution is necessary in this regard: Intense physical activity is a natural expression of the energy that junior youth possess. Experience worldwide has made clear that to favor, say, artistic activity over sports in a group begins a process of selection, in which some youth eventually feel reluctant to continue their participation.

- As in most other educational activities promoted by the Ruhi Institute, memorization of passages from the writings is to be given due importance in a program for the spiritual empowerment of junior youth. The question of memorization, then, needs to be a topic of conversation in one of the early meetings of the group. Animators should help the youth to become aware of the power of the Word of God, its effect on their lives, and the benefits of knowing many passages from the writings by heart.

- The question of language, of course, will have to be discussed to some extent before the youth begin their study of the first book, usually, as mentioned earlier, *Breezes of Confirmation*. In order to achieve higher and higher levels of intellectual and spiritual excellence, it can be explained, we need to develop our own powers of expression. We should be able to read and understand the meaning of what we have read, and we should learn to express our thoughts with clarity. Some animators ask the junior youth to enter into a serious pact: that they will listen to one another; that they will try to understand what each one of them means, even when he or she has difficulty expressing it; and that they will never make fun of what any one of them says. The group may, of course, have to be reminded gently of this pact every once in a while.

- In relation to the ability of reading well, a number of animators have encouraged junior youth to read the materials they study in their meetings, or other appropriate books, to children. Discussions that assist the members of the group in reflecting on this experience can deepen their awareness of the powers of expression.

With respect to all the points presented above, it is important to realize that, as animators gain experience, they are better able to assist junior youth in devising and carrying out activities that complement one another—activities which are a practical expression of the insights they have acquired through study of various texts and the high ideals they are striving to uphold.

# SECTION 31

From our discussions in the first and second units of this book, which were somewhat conceptual in nature, your preparations in this unit to serve as an animator of a junior youth group have taken on very practical dimensions. As you gain experience in this area of service, the pages of this book will continue to offer you ideas for reflection. Many animators find the points in the previous section particularly useful and refer to them again and again, maintaining a notebook in which they keep track of their experience and discussions with their fellow animators. In the meantime, it is suggested that you end this unit by reflecting on the implications of the endeavor on which you are now to embark. The words of the Universal House of Justice, addressed to older youth, are applicable to all those wishing to follow this path of service:

> "Not surprisingly, it is your age group that is gaining the most experience at aiding junior youth, and children too, with their moral and spiritual development, fostering in them capacity for collective service and true friendship. After all, aware of the world which these young souls will need to navigate, with its pitfalls and also its opportunities, you readily appreciate the importance of spiritual strengthening and preparation. Conscious, as you are, that Bahá'u'lláh came to transform both the inner life and external conditions of humanity, you are assisting those younger than yourselves to refine their characters and prepare to assume responsibility for the well-being of their communities. As they enter adolescence, you are helping them to enhance their powers of expression, as well as enabling a strong moral sensibility to take root within them. In so doing, your own sense of purpose is becoming more clearly defined as you heed Bahá'u'lláh's injunction: 'Let deeds, not words, be your adorning.'" [51]

# REFERENCES

1. From an unpublished letter dated 11 June 2006 written on behalf of the Universal House of Justice to an individual believer.

2. From an unpublished letter dated 19 July 2006 written on behalf of the Universal House of Justice to two individual believers.

3. From a letter dated 17 April 1936 written on behalf of Shoghi Effendi to an individual believer, published in *Directives from the Guardian* (New Delhi: Bahá'í Publishing Trust, 1973), p. 84.

4. 'Abdu'l-Bahá, in *Bahá'í Education: A Compilation of Extracts from the Bahá'í Writings,* compiled by the Research Department of the Universal House of Justice (London: Bahá'í Publishing Trust, 1998), pp. 28–29.

5. *The Promulgation of Universal Peace: Talks Delivered by 'Abdu'l-Bahá during His Visit to the United States and Canada in 1912* (Wilmette: Bahá'í Publishing, 2012), p. 471.

6. Ibid., p. 125.

7. From a talk given by 'Abdu'l-Bahá as reported by Ethel J. Rosenberg, cited by J. E. Esslemont, *Bahá'u'lláh and the New Era: An Introduction to the Bahá'í Faith* (Wilmette: Bahá'í Publishing, 2006, 2011 printing), p. 101.

8. *The Promulgation of Universal Peace*, p. 123.

9. Ibid., p. 204.

10. 'Abdu'l-Bahá, *Some Answered Questions* (Wilmette: Bahá'í Publishing Trust, 1984, 2009 printing), p. 300.

11. *Tablets of Abdul-Baha Abbas* (New York: Bahá'í Publishing Committee, 1915, 1940 printing), vol. 2, p. 276. (authorized translation)

12. *Khitábát: Talks of 'Abdu'l-Bahá* (Hofheim-Langenhain: Bahá'í-Verlag, 1984), pp. 131–32. (authorized translation)

13. *The Promulgation of Universal Peace*, p. 124.

14. *Paris Talks*, p. 113.

15. *Abdul Baha on Divine Philosophy* (Boston: The Tudor Press, 1918), p. 30.

16. *Selections from the Writings of 'Abdu'l-Bahá* (Wilmette: Bahá'í Publishing Trust, 1997, 2009 printing), no. 24, p. 57.

17. *Tablets of Abdul-Baha Abbas* (New York: Bahá'í Publishing Committee, 1909, 1930 printing), vol. 1, p. 63. (authorized translation)

18. *Selections from the Writings of 'Abdu'l-Bahá*, no. 155, p. 191.

19. 'Abdu'l-Bahá, *The Secret of Divine Civilization* (Wilmette: Bahá'í Publishing, 2007), p. 83.

20. *Tablets of Abdul-Baha Abbas*, vol. 1, pp. 71–72.

21. *Selections from the Writings of 'Abdu'l-Bahá*, no. 97, p. 133.

22. *Tablets of Bahá'u'lláh Revealed after the Kitáb-i-Aqdas* (Wilmette: Bahá'í Publishing Trust, 1988, 2005 printing), p. 72.

23. *The Proclamation of Bahá'u'lláh to the Kings and Leaders of the World* (Haifa: Bahá'í World Centre, 1967, 1978 printing), p. 78.

24. *Gleanings from the Writings of Bahá'u'lláh* (Wilmette: Bahá'í Publishing, 2005), no. 43, p. 104.

25. *The Promulgation of Universal Peace*, pp. 648–49.

26. *Tablets of Bahá'u'lláh Revealed after the Kitáb-i-Aqdas*, p. 143.

27. Ibid., p. 172.

28. *Tablets of Abdul-Baha Abbas*, vol. 1, p. 31. (authorized translation)

29. Ibid., p. 194. (authorized translation)

30. Bahá'u'lláh, *Epistle to the Son of the Wolf* (Wilmette: Bahá'í Publishing Trust, 1988, 2001 printing), p. 12.

31. *Tablets of Bahá'u'lláh Revealed after the Kitáb-i-Aqdas*, p. 172.

32. Ibid., pp. 172–73.

33. Ibid., p. 199.

34. *Gleanings from the Writings of Bahá'u'lláh*, no. 18, p. 47.

35. *Prayers and Meditations by Bahá'u'lláh* (Wilmette: Bahá'í Publishing Trust, 2013), no. 32, pp. 33–34.

36. *The Tabernacle of Unity: Bahá'u'lláh's Responses to Mánikchí Ṣáḥib and Other Writings* (Haifa: Bahá'í World Centre, 2006), p. 4.

37. *The Promulgation of Universal Peace*, p. 130.

38. *Prayers and Meditations*, no. 113, pp. 158–59.

39.  Bahá'u'lláh, in *Bahá'í Prayers: A Selection of Prayers Revealed by Bahá'u'lláh, the Báb, and 'Abdu'l-Bahá* (Wilmette: Bahá'í Publishing Trust, 2002, 2011 printing), p. 184.

40.  *Prayers and Meditations*, no. 178, pp. 248–49.

41.  Ibid., no. 79, p. 109.

42.  Bahá'u'lláh, in *Bahá'í Prayers*, p. 224.

43.  'Abdu'l-Bahá, in ibid., p. 249.

44.  Ibid., p. 28.

45.  Bahá'u'lláh, in ibid., p. 186.

46.  The Báb, in ibid., p. 189.

47.  'Abdu'l-Bahá, in ibid., pp. 200–1.

48.  *Prayers and Meditations*, no. 91, p. 128.

49.  From a message dated 12 December 2011 written by the Universal House of Justice to all National Spiritual Assemblies, published in *The Five Year Plan, 2011–2016: Messages of the Universal House of Justice* (West Palm Beach: Palabra Publications, 2013), p. 79.

50.  Ibid., pp. 79–80.

51.  From a message dated 1 July 2013 written by the Universal House of Justice to the participants in the forthcoming 114 youth conferences throughout the world, in ibid., pp. 106–7.